Interventions

Advances in Art and Urban Futures Volume 4

Edited by Malcolm Miles and Tim Hall

intellect ™
BRISTOL, ENGLAND
PORTLAND, OR, USA

First Published in 2005 by
Intellect Books, PO Box 862, Bristol, BS99 1DE, UK

First Published in USA in 2005 by
Intellect Books, ISBS, 5824 Hassalo St, Portland, Oregon 97213-3644, USA

Consulting Editor: Masoud Yazdoni
Book and Cover Design: Joshua Beadon – Toucan
Copy Editor: Holly Spradling

Set in Joanna

A catalogue record for this book is available from the British Library

ISBN 1-84150-118-2

ISSN 1742-9412 (Print)

Printed and bound in Great Britain by Antony Rowe Ltd.

Contents

Laurie Palmer

Acknowledgements

The Editors wish to express their thanks to all contributors; and to Josh Beadon of Toucan Design, Exeter for designing the book.

Chapter 7 describes a project funded by the Arts & Humanities Research Board (AHRB). Chapters 11 and 12 have arisen from evaluation research projects also funded by AHRB, at the University of Plymouth and the University of Gloucestershire respectively.

Thanks are due, also, to the Faculty of Arts at the University of Plymouth which has supported several seminars at which papers revised for publication in this volume were first given; and to the University of Barcelona, Carnegie Mellon University, and Bristol Legible City for hosting further events from which papers have been derived.

Interventions

Introduction

This is the fourth volume of collected papers in the series Advances in Art and Urban Futures. It follows *Cultures & Settlements* (edited by Malcolm Miles and Nicola Kirkham, 2003), and maintains the intention to bring together the perspectives of academics in several disciplines, artists, and other professionals involved in various ways in shaping contemporary cities. It maintains, too, a geographical breadth, with contributions in this volume from the USA, Germany, and Lithuania as well as the UK; and from UK contributors material on India, the Baltic states, and Barcelona. While most of the material relates to urban conditions and cultures, this volume includes a chapter on a rural arts project in Scotland. This offers a contrasting scenario through which at least the urban is seen more clearly via the contrast; it offers as well a reminder that significant cultural formations take place outside major centres of population. Of course, the intention is usually to remould the conditions of cultural production and reception, and in selecting papers for inclusion the editors have looked for critiques and case studies which state or imply such an aim. At the same time, wary of the difficulty of too easily accepting a model of cause and effect, they have included a paper which critically discusses instrumentality on the part of artists and arts organisations.

The book is organised in three sections: Policies and Strategies, Projects, and Evaluations. The first section addresses the arts and cultural policies, the strategies of cultural intermediaries and entrepreneurs in major cities including London, Mumbai, and Bristol. It includes a paper, in largely visual form, demonstrating a tactical game designed to elucidate the processes of decision-making facing shrinking, post-industrial cities. The papers are topical, dealing with, *inter alia*, issues of gentrification, cultural re-coding of urban neighbourhoods, public art policy, and depopulation from the loss of industries and its impact on perceptions of a city's future. Tania Carson critically reviews the cultural plan for London under its elected mayor. While the published strategy concerns culture in its broadest and most inclusive sense, Carson concludes that spatial planning is inevitably a controlling mechanism, in this case hiding social problems under a veneer of affluence denoted by culture. Andrew Harris extends the critique of culturally led redevelopment, looking more to the private sector and to Mumbai (Bombay, the site of Bollywood). He finds Indian entrepreneurs taking up the model of, say, SoHo in New York and Hoxton in London – in which art galleries and other cultural insertions in a run down neighbourhood serve to polarise wealth and poverty. In course of his investigations he casts new light on Sharon Zukin's work on loft living in SoHo. Alastair Snow writes from the viewpoint of a local authority officer (and performance artist, known previously for his guerrilla tactics). He looks in detail at policies for public art in Bristol, a city which has a revitalised harbour district housing a number of cultural institutions. He links this to the re-branding of Bristol as a 'legible city', and emphasises the role of consultation in defining appropriate public policies. Finally in this section, Friedrich von Borries and Matthias Böttger, writing from a perspective of architectural and urban design, present a game in which notional citizens participate in re-visioning their city. The focus is the shrinking city of Halle in the ex-East Germany, typical of many cities from which older, heavy industries have departed while the promise of newer, usually high-tech or knowledge-based industries has not as yet been realised. What is said of Halle could as easily apply to Pittsburgh or Middlesbrough.

Section Two looks at a range of projects and programmes in which artists intervene in urban (and in one case rural) sites. It combines descriptive and critical writing to construct a debate from which we might learn that there is no ideal model for intervention and that local conditions retain a degree of imperviousness to global scenarios. In some cases the projects seek to be regenerative; in others they problematise concepts such as culture and development. Ben Campkin scrutinises a project in London's Kings Cross area and its relation to the idea of legibility. He contextualises it in terms of a changing urban landscape and looks in detail at specific works. These tend to be specific not so much to a geographical site as to a set of conditions and to be temporary. He concludes with a cautionary note, that cultural re-branding of a neighbourhood can bypass its social needs or ignore its social complexities. Esther Salamon writes as an arts intermediary and consultant on an ambitious project (yet to be fully realised) linking post-industrial sites in the north-east of England, Latvia and Sweden. The sites define a Baltic territory in which heavy industry is depleted and some settlements left without the activity on which they were founded. As well as celebrating socio-economic histories, the project seeks to work within processes of identity formation. Perhaps one factor which artists can introduce in such situations is visibility, particularly for the everyday histories which are often overlooked in more glamorous or official media. Anne Douglas writes, in contrast, about an arts project in the north-east of Scotland, in rural Aberdeenshire. Here settlements comprise a few houses and farms, presenting an artist with a social fabric quite different from that of a city, in this case a resilient fabric despite pressures for depopulation. She emphasises individual participation and creative risk and the sharing of perceptions as well as transfer of skills. This is followed by a paper by Sheffield-based artists Andy Hewitt and Mel Jordan, whose work operates in the interstices of urban redevelopment. For instance, a space in a redundant industrial building typical of the kind converted into lofts to attract a new bohemian class to areas of economic decline is transformed into a simulated new apartment. The artists write that they do not build a last (romantic) barricade against capitalism but use art's experimental aspect to construct a space in which the influence of capital is nonetheless questioned. Laima Kreivyte, next, gives a summary of developments in non-gallery art in Lithuania since the late 1980s – since, that is, the dismantling of the Berlin Wall, end of the cold war and beginning of a liberalisation of the east bloc. In Lithuania, as in other Baltic states, this allows a resurgent nationalism intertwined with post-communism. The projects exhibit, variously, a post-modern irony, an understanding of feminism and the space of the body, and a concern for unselected public participation. In one case, rave culture intersects institutional culture. In another artists use public transport as their arena. Finally in this section, Laurie Palmer, a member of the artists' group Haha in Chicago, writes critically about instrumentality – the idea that artists (or planners, developers and cultural intermediaries) might intervene in a way which relies on a model of cause (the art policy or project) and effect (the fantasised revitalised city, for instance). It is very difficult to relinquish this model – even editing such a book as this assumes a degree of instrumentality in bringing the papers it contains to a public readership in order to inform future discussion. Palmer addresses the issue through specific projects carried out by Haha, and argues for acceptance of an element of unpredictability which keeps the outcomes of an intervention open. In a way, this is compatible with Adorno's retention of a creative tension between polarities (such as art's aesthetic and social dimensions) – the effort being always to keep the discussion open, to avoid closure at any price.

The third section includes two papers on art in non-gallery sites, one reporting the findings of a comparative evaluation, the other outlining the basis from which a current evaluative project sets out. Both evaluations were funded by the Arts and Humanities Research Board. There is a general lack of critical material assessing the outcomes of arts projects or which seeks to understand their impact for differing groups. Sara Selwood's *The Benefits of Public Art* (1985, London, Policy Studies Institute) remains a seminal work, its title turning out to be somewhat ironic in relation to its content. But nearly ten years on, in a changed academic and cultural climate, these two studies provide new material on both non-gallery art projects *and* the ways in which they can appropriately be evaluated. The scope of both projects is far more limited than Selwood's study across three English regions, yet they offer insights into the reception of local initiatives which may inform future debate. As to what future projects, or more accurately their protagonists, will learn from such insights, as editors we decline prediction. All we can say is that – in face of sometimes staggering claims made in both the private and public sectors for art as an agent of regeneration – the knowledges and experiences of those in whose spaces art intervenes require as much consideration as the knowledges of the professionals who make such interventions. Among necesary considerations will be, too, a deconstruction of the idea that art is instrumental in urban change – a discussion opened in Palmer's paper in Section Two and which may lead to further research.

■ Contributors

Tania Carson is a graduate student at London Metropolitan University, and previously completed a degree in Social Science (Anthropology) at Stokholm University.

Andrew Harris is a doctoral student at University College London (Geography) and has carried out field work in London and Mumbai.

Alastair Snow is Public Art Officer for Bristol City Council, was previously Director of Cleveland Arts and has a background in performance art.

Friedrich von Borries and Matthias Bottger are architects and spatial technicians (Raumtaktiker) working in Berlin. Their work, BurgerMeister, will be played in different shrinking cities in 2004 – www.raumtaktik.de

Ben Campkin teaches at the Bartlett School of Architecture, UCL, and is Deputy Editor of the journal City: *Analysis of Urban Trends, Culture, Theory, Policy, Action.*

Esther Salamon is an arts consultant working on socially responsive projects in the northeast of England and coordinator of Cargo. She teaches at Durham University.

Anne Douglas is Senior Research Fellow at Grays School of Art, Robert Gordon University, Aberdeen.

Andy Hewitt and Mel Jordan are artists whose practice is defined by its political and social engagement through specific sites; they teach at the University of Wolverhapton and live in Sheffield.

Laime Kreivyte is a doctoral student in Vilnius, studying the development 0f non-gallery art in Lithuania.

Laurie Palmer is a member of the artists' group Haha in Chicago.

Sarah Bennett is a doctoral student at the University of Plymouth and Principal Lecturer in sculpture.

John Butler is Chair of Art at the Birmingham Art Institute, University of Central England, and President of the European League of Institutes of Art.

Nicola Kirkham is a doctoral student at Central St Martin's College of Art and Design, London Institute, researching activism.

Malcolm Miles is Reader in Cultural Theory at the University of Plymouth.

Tim Hall is Senior Lecturer in Geography at the University of Gloucestershire.

Chereen Smith is a postgraduate student in the School of Environment, University of Gloucestershire. She was formerly a research assistant at the University of Gloucestershire and currently works in rural regeneration in the South West of England.

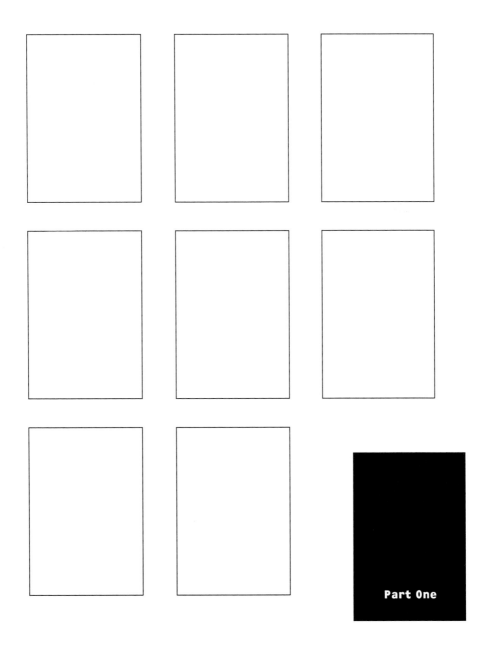

Part One

Policies and Strategies

Tania Carson

Cultural Ambiguity in an Urban Development Master Plan. Deception or Miscalculation?

`Culture' is the latest buzz word in urban planning. In the British Prime Minister Tony Blair's popularised version of politics, the former Tory emphasis on Heritage Britain has been replaced with New Labour's Creative Britain, whereby the creative industries are marketed as the major source of economic expansion' (GLAb, 2002:5). Bringing culture to the people is a favourite theme of New Labour (a neologism of the Labour government elected in 1997 with Tony Blair as Prime Minister). The creation of the Department of Culture, Media and Sport (DCMS) and the establishment of the Greater London Authority (GLA) were two initiatives aimed at distinguishing Blair from his predecessors. Whereas Margaret Thatcher had been responsible for dismantling the Greater London Council (GLC) in 1986, thereby putting an end to strategic planning in London and diminishing the government's attention to the arts, the GLA hopes to re-address these issues. It unites the thirty-two London boroughs and the Corporation of London. It is composed of an elected mayor, Ken Livingstone, and a separately elected assembly. The Mayor is responsible for strategic planning in the city. Lately, culture has had a vital role to play within urban regeneration schemes. It is marketed as important in tackling crime and social exclusion and in restoring the nation's failing health. Livingstone, like his former Barcelona counterpart Pascual Maragall, is using culture-led regeneration schemes to project himself as powerful and reforming. In many ways, theorizing around culture has also been substituted for the former public arts dialogue. These days culture has a tough reputation to live up to.

Livingstone has devised a number of strategies for improving London, amongst them the *Culture Strategy*, published earlier this year. He has also drawn up a proposal for the first London-wide masterplan for twenty years, the *Draft London Plan*. Both the *Plan* and the *Strategy* are still in draft form and are currently being reviewed by inspectors. It claims that the '[d]esignation, development and management of cultural quarters can help address the need for affordable workspace for creative industries, provide flexible live/work space, encourage clusters of activity and provide a trigger for local regeneration' (GLAa, 2002:207). This comes under the section heading of 'Development and Promotion of Arts and Culture' (GLAa, 2002: 206) which deals with the development of cultural quarters, in particular in deprived areas, where they should be 'sustained by the planning system and supported by wider economic and cultural development initiatives' (GLAa, 2002: 207). The *Plan* is to replace the regional planning guidances, the *Unitary Development Plans* (UDP), that each borough devises for its area. It will provide general design and planning guidance with which local boroughs are expected to produce plans in 'general conformity' (GLAa, 2002: v).

But what exactly is culture? The *Culture Strategy* makes it clear that it is 'about culture in its broadest sense, encapsulating areas as diverse as creative industries and sport, green space and museums' (GLAc, 2003: 10-11). Within anthropological discourse, the idea of culture is more or less interchangeable with the activities of daily life. The *Strategy* claims to promote a diverse and varied culture but it offers only a monotone prescriptive culture by its focus on venues, events and contrived cultural quarters. Whereas previously culture was reserved for the middle and upper classes, now it is sold as accessible to all classes who have more spending money and more free time. The theory behind this notion of culture accessible to everyone is that it is a basic 'right'. This implies, however, that it is only the prescribed entertainment and associated licensing laws and infrastructure, the *planned* culture, which is accessible as a right. In turn, this can mean the loss of spontaneity within real life authentic spaces. Already in the late forties, Theodor Adorno and Max Horkheimer used the term 'culture industry' to designate the products and processes of mass culture, which they held responsible for producing cultural homogeneity and predictability (Storey, 1993: 100). Today, culture has become synonymous with *entertainment* for the masses, yet it is promoted as a vehicle to improve London as a 'world-class' city.

The government pays homage to access, diversity and excellence in its mission to recreate London as a world-class city of culture. In a climate where the definition of culture is becoming more and more elusive, culture in its many guises has infiltrated most aspects of our daily lives. But culture is contested. Anthropologists have been tackling the idea of culture since they began studying the practices of other peoples and societies. In the initial stages of the discipline the idea of culture was straightforward. It was something that could be studied, described and even judged. It was the 'other'. Now, culture is seen not only as a way of living but also as the *source* of the explanation, the reason why people act and live and think as they do. Whereas anthropologists might recognize that an understanding of culture as habit, beliefs and traditions might indeed aid in resolving society's problems, the government's adamant marketing of the benefits of culture is of a narrower definition. Even within anthropological discourse the definitions of culture vary. Generally it is viewed as either being vernacular, as something which cannot be understood from outside its own realm, or as a universal law, similar to a language. Despite its insistence otherwise, the government is primarily concerned with culture as 'high art' but wants to bring it 'down' to 'the people'. Culture is something you do. Ultimately, it is something consumed, whether it be visiting an art gallery, going to an event or joining in a sports activity.

Culture is also valued as a supposed catalyst for regeneration. The object of regeneration is economic, social, political and cultural renewal. Urban regeneration is defined as the 'comprehensive and integrated vision and action that leads to the resolution of urban problems and which seeks to bring about lasting improvement in the economic, physical, social and environmental conditions of an area that has been or is subject to change' (Roberts and Sykes, 2000: 17). Both the *London Plan* and the DCMS view the arts as offering a major contribution to neighbourhood renewal. The former Secretary of State for Culture, Media and Sport, Chris Smith, maintains that the 'five principal reasons for state subsidy of the arts in the modern world [are] to ensure excellence; to protect innovation; to assist access for as many people as possible, both to create and appreciate; to help provide the seedbed for the creative economy; and to assist in the regeneration of areas of deprivation' (Smith quoted in Selwood, 2001: xlvi). This is reflected in the proposal that all boroughs should produce *Creative Strategies* (GLAb, 2002: 49) and in the DCMS insistence that the arts in society should not only contribute to neighbourhood renewal but should be accessible by as many people as possible (DCMS website). However, measuring the arts is problematic, in terms of governmental demands for accountability and excellence and of a demonstrable contribution to regeneration.

Regeneration exploits the city's wastelands and fringe. The dispossessed are marginalised, as are the artists who attracted the developers to the locality in the first place. There is a concern about who will benefit from regeneration schemes overall. Urban planners have a tendency to adopt a moralistic tone and equate redevelopment with social benefit (Deutsche, 1996: 66). This echoes the rhetoric used as an alibi for imperialism. 'If culture is to be protected...is it not precisely from those whose business it is to protect culture?' (Owens quoted in Deutsche, 1996: 291). Instead, urban planning should pay more consideration to issues relating to the real conservation and preservation of the environment. To what extent urban regeneration is actually culturally led is not clear. Much of the money comes from the European funding system which focuses on the arts infrastructure and limits direct intervention. It is concerned with regional aid and large-scale projects for economic gain. This is not arts planning but regional economic planning (Evans, 2001: 216).

The East End has been selected as 'the priority area for new development' (GLAa, 2002: 8) according to the forthcoming *London Plan*. It has a high proportion of artists, immigrants and refugees but maintains a position peripheral to the wider society. There are several schemes, however, to integrate it into the mainstream, both physically by railway and tube extensions and symbolically by the development of 'cultural quarters'. The creation of cultural quarters is merely a kind of cultural branding. The Brick Lane area, for example, is promoted as 'Banglatown', referencing its large Bangladeshi community, or as 'Eastside' in an attempt to market it as the eastern 'West End'. However, the surrounding Stepney remains one of the poorest areas in London with severe drug-related issues and problems with integration into the wider society. The East London Line Extension (ELLX) caused a dispute over the planned demolition of the old Bishopsgate Goodsyard. It is a structure dating from the mid-nineteenth century which remained closed for over thirty years after a fire only to be rediscovered by recently evicted businesses (*Spaces*, 2003: 3). It is one of the inner city's lost spaces but developers have now been given the go-ahead for demolition. The plans for an East London tube extension have existed since the Broadgate redevelopment in Moorgate in the eighties (Selwood, 1996: 99).

The East End is also heavily affected by the 'Gateway to the Continent' programmes, originally initiated in the early nineties by Michael Heseltine, a cabinet minister to Margaret Thatcher. Two artist collectives, SPACE (Space Provision, Artistic, Cultural and Educational) and Acme, were established in the seventies. They allocated studios for artists in properties earmarked for demolition or resale, leased to them temporarily by

No Ball Games, Hackney Road, London (photo Tania Carson)

Contesting Cultures, Hackney Road, London (photo Tania Carson)

Please Drive Carefully, Hackney Road, London (photo Tania Carson)

Acquired for Peanuts, Hackney Road, London (photo Tania Carson)

Dalston Lane, Hackney Road, London (photo Mitchell)

Seek, Hackney Road, London (photo Tania Carson)

the GLC (Wedd, 2001:142). The eighties property boom and changes in the legal enforcement of tenants' rights led to Acme moving into ex-industrial spaces, frequently in the East End because of its manufacturing and production history. But both SPACE and Acme and the artists they support have suffered at the hands of government promotion of culture. In 1972 the St. Katherine's Docks studios were sold to allow a hotel-complex redevelopment. In the late eighties the massive Carpenter's Road collective sponsored by Acme had to yield to a 'Gateway to the Continent' venture, namely, the Stratford Cross-Channel Rail Station (Wedd, 2001: 146). One of the more recent downsides of urban regeneration with respect to the arts can be seen with the demise of the initially *Arts Council* (ACE) funded Lux Centre in Hoxton Square. In four years it reputedly ran up a huge debt, leading to closure (*Art Monthly*, 2001: 15). Like St.Katherine's Docks and Carpenter's Road, it is a prime site for redevelopment.

The area around Spitalfields Market is facing a similar fate. The site is owned by the Corporation of London but its Tower Hamlets location gives the borough a say in determining its future. Tower Hamlets opted for redevelopment, sacrificing cultural diversity and tradition. Half of the old Horner Market-building has been demolished to give way to an office block designed by Norman Foster, to create 'desirable' public space (SMUT website). That the office block should have been designed by Foster comes as no surprise either. Amongst other projects, he has redesigned the controversial Great Court of the British Museum and won the competition for the equally problematic Millenium Bridge. His most recent project has been the transformation of Trafalgar Square, completed in July 2003, and he is a contender for the masterplanning of the Olympic Village. Six prestigious architectural firms are chasing the redevelopment contract, most notably: Herzog and de Meuron, Richard Rogers Partnership and Arup with, once again, Foster and Partners. Herzog and de Meuron are wellknown for the Tate Modern redevelopment at Bankside and for the Laban Dance *Centre* in Deptford; and Richard Rogers Partnership for the Dome. 'There can never have been a moment when quite so much high-visibility architecture has been designed by so few people. Sometimes it seems as if there are just thirty architects in the world' (Teedon, 2002: 56). The other half of the market is in the hands of Ballymore Plc, whose proposed redevelopment would impose a shopping mall and Camden pastiche street market, with exorbitant market-stall prices ousting traders and leaving nothing but chain-store retail outlets. This is allowed to happen despite the *Plan's* specific intention to '[e]nsure that local communities benefit from economic growth and are engaged in the development process' (GLAa, 2002:.10). Ken Livingstone has admitted that the renewal scheme 'will alter the social fabric of this unique locality', but will 'increase the supply of office space'(ESa, 2002: 22). Spitalfields is a prime example of the current conflicts between regeneration and the local community and the elusive role played by culture.

'The Mayor strongly supports an Olympic Games bid based on the lower Lea Valley in the Thames Gateway. This deprived area of East London is a priority area for the Mayor and his economic arm the LDA. Work is already underway to prepare a master plan for the potential Olympic infrastructure and transport in a way that will ensure the wider regeneration of the area' (GLAc,: 52). The Olympic Village will lead to increased privatization and rob the area of large open spaces. The site for the 2012 Olympics will not be decided until 2005, leaving seven years for preparation of the venues. This halts any other possible plans for the area. However, if, in fact, the Lower Lea Valley has been identified as an area in need of regeneration its renewal should not be dependent on a bid to host a large event. If London does get the Olympics, there will be issues of displacement and cultural homogenization, followed by problems of subsequent sustainment: tourist interest may be short-lived, leaving behind a high-profile masterplanned Olympic Village running up huge debts and maintenance costs. The Olympic Village runs the risk of becoming the new Millenium Dome. The Dome's architect, Richard Rogers, is Ken Livingstone's chief architectural adviser. Originally, it was a Tory initiative, promoted by Heseltine. In the 1997 change of government, New Labour decided to continue the Millenium project. It quickly became an expensive white elephant. The masterplanning creates superficial versions of real local culture to market to tourists and to aid in the promotion of London as a 'world-class' city.

The planning of arts and culture has existed for as long as the planning of towns and cities themselves, from the Athenian *polis* to Haussmann's Paris, but exactly which ones are worthy of planning programmes vary over time and space. It is assumed that planning results in positive change and that culture is a progressive catalyst for urban renewal. The origins of the current emphasis on culture-driven urban renewal are in the free-market revolution of the seventies and the discovery of the 'inner city' as a political issue. By the late sixties Britain's manufacturing economic base had fallen into decline, there was growing poverty and mounting racial tensions. Previously urban renewal had been concerned with regulating urban growth and providing housing away from the slums, on *greenfield* sites. By the seventies, however, the focus had shifted to new economic development and the revitalization of decaying inner cities. In 1968 the *Urban Programme*, administered by the Home Office, was introduced as a means of focusing on the needy areas of inner city slums. A few years later the Department of the Environment (DoE) took over responsibility for urban policies. A more economy-based view of urban deprivation was developed which abandoned the previous social-welfare approach (Roberts and Sykes, 2000:29). During this period the modernist plans encountered popular resistance, for example in Covent Garden, where the plan was accused of designing to 'blanket the area' (Hebbert, 1998: 84). The *Greater London Plan* was devised in 1976, and revised by Ken Livingstone in 1984. It sought to revive London's manufacturing base.

The Labour report *The Arts and the People*, focusing on community-based activities and inner city regeneration, was published the following year. The arts were promoted as a way to counteract crime and vandalism (Selwood, 1996: 22). Communal projects such as murals were supported in the hope of unifying deteriorating neighbourhoods. Today, these murals can be seen in rundown neighbourhoods where the real problems of poverty, lack of education, deprived health services and social exclusion are yet to be tackled. In 1979 the Labour government was replaced by the Conservatives and a new urban policy was deployed. Thatcher opposed the notion of the state being the main funding agent and promoted private sector investment with partnership regeneration schemes. Michael Heseltine, then Secretary of State for the DoE, was a keen advocate for government intervention on the side of entrepreneurs. He initiated the *Urban Development Corporations* (UDC) in derelict Merseyside, for example, and in 1981, established the now infamous London Dockland Development Corporation (LDDC). These Corporations were local, property-led regeneration schemes functioning within a prescribed time limit. Planning became synonymous with property development. They were the major innovation of Conservative urban development policy, quickly followed by the Urban Development Grant and Inner City Enterprise Zones to aid property development (Roberts and Sykes, 2000).

Meanwhile, the Arts Council of England (ACE) budget had been cut. But both the ACE and the GLC opposed Thatcherite values and campaigned for a more popular role for the arts. In 1986, after a period of inner strife and diminishing power, the GLC was finally dismantled, a major setback, it is claimed, to strategic planning (Risebero, 1996: 223). The only significant development in London during this period was in Docklands. In 1988 the Urban Regeneration Grant (initiated the year before to assist the private sector) and Urban Development Grant merged to form City Grant, awarded directly to developers without the previously required mediation of a local authority. Three years later, the City Challenge was introduced. It lasted for several years and required local authorities to bid competitively for funds with partners, abandoning the fixed allocation of funds. A mid-nineties study showed that City Challenge bidding winners in London had named partners within the private sector, unlike the losers, which was why the latter were denied funds (Florio and Brownhill, 2000: 57).

For the 1992 elections the Conservative government reviewed their urban policy and started two new schemes, the Private Finance Initiative (PFI) and the Single Regeneration Budget (SRB) (Miles, 1997: 59). The SRB worked in a similar way to City Challenge, forcing areas and cities to compete against each other for bids against criteria determined by the DoE. Urban policy became more local and project-based. Culture was no longer subsidy-reliant but a vehicle for gaining profit. Critics maintained that this system of awarding big funds to 'important' design-based schemes hid the fact that funds were being withdrawn from the general regeneration programme. '[U]rban regeneration became separated from the mainstream planning process...' (Hall, 1996: 409). In 1994, English Partnerships was created through the merger of English Estates, City Grant and Derelict Land Grant to promote the reclamation and redevelopment of derelict vacant and underused land and buildings (Symon and Williams, 2001: 57). Today, it is through the SRB, and the European Union, that most cultural projects receive funds, although it is difficult to determine how much of the overall sum is allocated to culture since a sum of money is given to the regeneration of the area as a whole.

Recently, the ACE and the Regional Arts Boards merged to form a single funding body. London Arts has produced a paper on the relationship between their organization and the local authorities. Funding is most likely to be allocated to the development of a leisure project, tourism or infrastructure. It still falls within the cultural sector in the guise of visitor attraction. Further on, the report states that support for the arts can be attracted through non-specific arts-orientated initiatives, such as education, regeneration and social inclusion. It estimates that theatre and arts in education are the areas which will receive increased funding next year (London Arts, 2002: 3). The current Funding Agreement between the DCMS and the ACE states that the main policy for the arts is access, excellence and education (DCMS website). New obligations make funding dependent on outcome (Selwood, 2001). Therefore, it becomes a concern that '[t]o sign on for state benefit, the arts must now pay lip-service to multiculturalism, education, equal opportunity and a range of objectives that have nothing to do with art' (ESb, 2002: 13). It is also contradictory that these bodies which allocate funds and have previously promoted public art are not held accountable to similar demands and have instead been transformed 'into ineffective commissioners with their own set of aesthetic preferences' (Fink, 2002: 27).

UK government policy is to develop on brownfield sites, in other words, any land or premises previously used or developed but currently disused. The government has initiated the Urban Task Force responsible for locating these areas of deprivation. The Barcelona model has become a standard recipe for redevelopment. Cultural quarters are planned in areas of perceived social deprivation and physical dilapidation. The transformation of cities only takes place in areas chosen to house the new and improved cultural, and historical, quarters. With this singling out of pockets of decay, and *perceived* cultural decay, local communities risk being ignored in favour of financial exploitation. Although referred to as areas suffering from neglect and social and economic depravation, it is not always the case that the *most* needy areas are actually chosen for the cultural-led regeneration. It is these often prolific high-profile design-schemes, with the usual top firms short listed, that results in the spectacle of 'signature architecture'. Furthermore, the needs of the local area are not automatically addressed by large-scale cultural projects and flagship developments (Foord and Evans, 2000: 249). 'Even in the most fêted examples of regeneration and cities of culture, these strategic planning solutions…in fact reinforce the divided city at the cost of local amenities and genuine mixed-use of buildings and sites…' (Evans, 2001: 17). This trend of creating 'cultural quarters' in rundown areas leads to cities across the globe looking more like each other. Like the financial enclaves, such as Docklands built in the eighties and early nineties in 'deprived' areas, these 'cultural quarters' do not always have anything in common with the neighbourhoods in the immediate vicinity. Visual strategies and designed elements function to increase social polarization. Urban planners also forget that the desired 'quarters' cannot be constructed by cold planning, only by the people who live and use these areas.

The objective of urban planning is to create a unified package of the city based on good design and aesthetics. Paradoxically, despite its intentions to consider all aspects of culture, the government advocates only a narrower view which limits the possibilities for participating in and perceiving cultural diversity. The homogenous cultural city aims to design-out aspects incompatible with the city-image. In the shift from strategies advocating greenfield growth for the purpose of housing people to strategies concerned with the renewal of brownfield sites close to the city centre, the emphasis is on design and image, not on planning. In fact, the master plans which are in vogue now are reminiscent of previous utopian and totalitarian visions. They used urban planning and architecture as a tool to destroy chaotic urban space and disorder. Through hierarchies of space and city layouts enforcing segregation, the master planners sought to create a 'perfect' world. Spatial planning is a form of social control. Anything or anyone undesired would simply not exist, or in any case, not be seen. 'In the city of reason, there were no winding roads, no cul-de-sacs and no unattended sites left to chance – and thus no vagabonds, vagrants or nomads' (Bauman quoted in Calow, 2002: 119). Similarly, in the regenerated city, appearance is everything. Social problems are hidden behind a façade of affluence and culture. Official public spaces are created at the expense of the vibrancy of the streets and the bustle of ordinary life. The propaganda tone of culture-led regeneration schemes avoids addressing the need for the conservation of authentic space.

Bibliography

Art Monthly No.251, Nov. 2001

Calow, J. (2002) 'From Birmingham to Bogota' in Rugg, J. and Hinchcliffe, D. (eds.) Recoveries and Reclamations: Advances in art and urban future, vol. 2 Bristol and Portland: Intellect.

Deutsche, R. (1996) Eviction: Art and Spatial Politics Massachusetts: Mass. Inst. of Technology.

Evans, G. (2001) Cultural Planning: An urban renaissance? London and New York: Routledge.

ESa The Evening Standard (11/10/02) Bar-Hillel, M. 'Celebrities join last-ditch battle to save Spitalfields'.

ESb The Evening Standard (11/10/02) Lebrecht, N. 'Can anyone see the next big thing?'

Fink (2002) in Art and Architecture: Next Generation November 2002, Art and Architecture, Journal n0.57 supplement.

Florio, S. and Brownhill, S. (2001) 'Whatever happened to Criticism? Interpreting the London Docklands Development Corporation's obituary' in Catterall, B. (ed) City: Analysis of Urban trends, culture, theory, policy, action vol.4, no.1, April 2000.

Ford, J. and Evans, G. (2000) 'Landscapes of cultural production and regeneration' in Benson, J.F. and Roe, M. (eds.) Urban Lifestyles: Spaces, places, people Rotterdam: Balkema.

GLAa The Draft London Plan: Draft Spatial Development Strategy for Greater London London: GLA, June 2002.

GLAb Creativity: London's Core Business London: GLA, September 2002.

GLAc The Mayor's Draft Culture Strategy London: GLA, June 2003. The Guardian, G2 (02/06/03), p.2ff, Beckett, A. 'Can culture save us?'

Hall, P. (1996) Cities of Tomorrow. Oxford and Cambridge, MA.: Blackwell.

Hebbert, M. (1998) London: More by fortune than design London: Wiley & Sons Ltd.

London Arts (2002) Working with Local Authorities London: London Arts.

Miles, M. (1997) Art, Space and the City, London, Routledge.

Risebero (1996) in Butler, T. and Rustin, M. (eds.) Rising in the East? The regeneration of East London London: Lawrence and Wishart.

Roberts, P. and Sykes, H. (2000) (eds.) Urban Regeneration: A Handbook London, New Delhi and Thousand Oaks: SAGE.

Spaces The Hackney Society: Issue 13, Winter 2003.

Selwood, S. (1996) *The Benefits of Public Art: The Polemics of permanent art in public places* London: PSI.

Selwood (2001) in Selwood, S. (ed.) *The U.K. Culture Sector: Profile and policy issues* London: PSI.

Storey, J. (1993) *An Introductory Guide to Cultural Theory and Popular Culture* Hertfordshire: Harvester and Wheatsheaf.

Symon and Williams in Selwood, S. (2001) (ed.) *The U.K. Culture Sector: Profile and policy issues* London: PSI.

Teedon, P. 'New Urban Spaces' (2002) in Rugg, J. and Hinchcliffe, D. (eds.) *Recoveries and Reclamations: Advances in art and urban future, vol.2* Bristol and Portland: Intellect.

Wedd, K. (2001) *Creative Quarters: The art world in London 1700-2000* London: Merrell.

DCMS website www.culture.gov.uk

Spitalfields Market Under Threat website www.smut.org.uk

Andrew Harris

Opening Up the Symbolic Economy of Contemporary Mumbai

I am standing at the back of the cavernous former turbine hall in London's Tate Modern during their *Century City* exhibition in 2001. Again and again I am drawn to one artwork on the far wall. Three large metal storefront shutters, each with a black-and-white portrait of a child on its crenulated surfaces are wound up, or down, by the Tate attendant every twenty minutes or so. Directly behind the shutters are bright collage-like paintings merging elements of hectic, everyday streetlife with floating images of film stars, politicians and religious leaders. This shutter triptych, by Atul Dodiya, entitled *Missing*, is part of the Bombay/Mumbai section of the exhibition, representing, along with London, the cultural trajectories of the last decade of the twentieth century. The dynamic and striking visual culture conveyed by Dodiya's shutters leads me to consider how contemporary Mumbai relates to arguments about the increasing importance of the urban symbolic economy. How is art being used as a 'shopfront' for contemporary Mumbai? In what ways does Mumbai differ from the increasing aestheticisation of the built environment in other cities such as New York? This essay examines the particularities of the role of contemporary art in Mumbai, focusing on one area, Lower Parel, which many predict will soon resemble the art district of SoHo in New York. By comparing and contrasting Lower Parel to SoHo, the chapter looks to open up both the complexities and specificities of Mumbai's symbolic economy and the Eurocentric assumptions of urban research.[1]

It is no surprise that Mumbai (the name was changed officially from Bombay in 1995) was chosen by the Tate Gallery's curators to represent the closing years of the twentieth century. The Population Institute in Washington D.C. forecast that Mumbai will be the world's largest urban agglomeration by 2015, with a population of over twenty-eight million. And it seems to be displaying the typical contemporary metamorphosis of the capitalist city, shedding its traditional industrial base and relying on expanded financial and cultural sectors: the share of employment in manufacturing industries in Greater Mumbai declined from 36% in 1980 to 28.5% in 1990, whereas trade, finance and service industries have increased their share of employment from 52.1% to 64.3% in the same period (BMRDA, 1995). But Mumbai is not simply an important city in terms of its size and rapid restructuring. It occupies an increasingly central role in relation to global economic and cultural flows. The liberalisation and deregulation of the Indian economy in 1991 has opened Mumbai up to greater global traffic, with the city reaffirming its role, established during the colonial era, as the subcontinent's main gateway for the wider world. Virtually all the 295 foreign institutional investors that have flocked to India since 1991 have set up in Mumbai (Nicholson, 1995). And from the current craze for the electronic sampling of Bombay's Bollywood film-scores by major American hip-hop and Jamaican dancehall producers, to the London-based musical *Bombay Dreams*, or the literature of Salman Rushdie and Rohinton Mistry, Mumbai increasingly infiltrates the popular cultural imaginations of other world cities. It is now an archetypal 'post-modern' metropolis of commerce, finance and culture (Masselos, 1995).

Contemporary art in Mumbai is itself an illustration of the city's recent restructuring and its increasingly important role on the global stage. Rooted in the city's former British ruling society, contemporary art has blossomed over the past fifteen years. Whereas in 1981 there were only two genuine sponsoring galleries in Bombay, plus two smaller commission galleries and less than half-a-dozen rental galleries (Ty-Tomkins Seth, 1981: 113), today there are approximately forty-five, including a branch of the Indian National Gallery of Modern Art which opened in 1996. As one enthusiastic journalist recently exclaimed, 'Mumbai has never had it better as far as the art world is concerned. To say that the art scene in the city is perking up is putting it mildly' (Ninan, 2000). Significantly, this growth of Mumbai's art world derives not only from domestic demand and investment but has also been shaped by international interest. The entry of Christie's and Sotheby's auction houses into Mumbai's art scene from 1995, together with the purchasing power of non-resident Indians in cities such as New York, Toronto, London and Dubai has placed Mumbai's art world firmly on a global map. The inclusion of Mumbai in the *Century City* is a further part of this process, and one that hints at the parallels between Mumbai and a city such as London. From the upstairs galleries of the Tate Modern during the exhibition, it was possible to look down at 1990s Mumbai juxtaposed next to 1990s London in the vast space of the former turbine hall. Atul Dodiya's bright, and noisy, shutters at one end of the hall stood out against a glass case displaying a selection of private viewing cards for London galleries at the other. Maybe the US Deputy Secretary of State, Lawrence Summers, was correct to speculate in 1997 that the American magazine *Vanity Fair* would be declaring Mumbai, not London, 'the world's coolest city' (D'Monte, 2002: 51).

Such a comparison to London is one that many elite groups in Mumbai are keen to encourage. The transnational practices and sensibilities of visual arts are seen as an important way of aligning Mumbai with international notions of the creative city. This is part of the rationale behind the creation in 1999 of an annual arts festival in a central precinct of the city called Kala Ghoda for ten days in February. With its pavement galleries, cultural performances and exhibitions, set in and around a bold ensemble of neo-Gothic colonial architecture, the organisers are eager to place the festival within a global continuum. One of its co-ordinators talks of how the Kala Ghoda festival 'sooner or later will be on the map; you will travel to Salzburg [in Austria] in August and I think people will come to Bombay in February.' Indeed, many of the artists involved are international, such as the German street-band that performed in 2003 or the Picasso Exhibition that was the centrepiece of the 2002 festival. With this Western orientation, the space of Kala Ghoda is a way for particular social groups in Mumbai to assert the globally competitive ambitions of the city. This is why the local media regularly frame the area's potential in relation to cultural districts such as Covent Garden in London or Paris's Latin Quarter (e.g. Balaram, 1998).

Another area of Mumbai that has drawn comparisons with districts in other major global cities through an association with contemporary art is Lower Parel. For over a century, Lower Parel has been the industrial heart of Mumbai, filled with composite textile mills and crowded workers' housing and markets. However, its prime location in the very centre of Mumbai's narrow peninsular, well-served by transport links, has encouraged many millowners to redevelop their land in ways that respond to Mumbai's new post-liberalisation economic landscape. Textile production has been shifted to small-scale, unregulated powerlooms and handlooms in Mumbai's burgeoning suburbs and many of Lower Parel's mills have been converted into luxury apartments and office space. This remaking of the area has involved art-related activities and imaginaries; most notably the reuse of a disused tool storage shed in Shree Ram Mills by the Sakshi Gallery. This gallery opened in 1997 with an inaugural show entitled SPIN (Sakshi Presents Images of the Nineties), referencing both the gallery's previous association with textile manufacture and the way its location was a bold turnaround of traditional notions of viewing art in Mumbai. Sakshi's recycling of industrial space, its deliberate reuse of industrial fixtures and fittings in its architectural conversion and its encouragement of larger-scale experimental art-pieces has led to comparisons with SoHo in downtown Manhattan, New York, where a precedent was set for the transformation of manufacturing premises into raw art spaces in the 1960s and 1970s (Simpson, 1981). In an article entitled *Slow Steps to SoHo*, Patel (1998) speculates how the opening of the Sakshi could herald a new art-filled era for Lower Parel, quoting the painter Mehlli Gobhai who posits Sakshi as 'the first breakthrough of the SoHo kind in Mumbai'. This 'promise of a new SoHo' (Hoskote, 1998) was reinforced in 2002 when another of Shree Ram's sheds was transformed into a nightclub, complete with large sculptures made from redundant metal scrap.

SoHo similarly looms over some of the attempts to provide a guiding master plan for the redevelopment of Lower Parel's mills. In his 1996 report on the future of Lower Parel's nationally-owned mills, the internationally renowned Indian architect Charles Correa recommended that the printing department at Kohinoor Mill, the engine room at Sitaram Mill and various parts of Tata Mill could all be turned into art galleries, a vision that has been described as 'SoHo meets Canary Wharf' (Paradkar, 1997: 40). Others have suggested that workers' housing could be redeveloped as artists' studios (Balaram, 1996) while a display in the Bombay/Mumbai section of *Century City* proposed that several of Lower Parel's mill structures are:

> Robust enough to be recycled as studios for artists ... Thus would come into being a new centre for Bombay in the heart of the city with its distinctive ambience – a centre which adds another dimension to this vital metropolis. [2]

Such a statement shows how activities associated with contemporary art are viewed by many in Mumbai to be an important part of the remoulding of the city's once thriving mill-lands, enabling the area to emulate, or indeed rival, the successes of other formerly industrial areas such as SoHo.

Lower Parel in the foreground with downtown Mumbai in the distance (photo Shehkar Krishnan)

Derelict mill buildings near the Sakshi Gallery, Lower Parel (photo Matthew Gandy)

An example of a **Chawl** (workers' housing) in Lower Parel (photo Andrew Harris)

SoHo could be found at the Tate's *Century City*. It featured as part of 'New York 1969-1974', the section immediately preceding Mumbai and London chronologically. Several photographs of SoHo rooftops and derelict buildings were displayed, signifying not only the importance of this locality as the setting and inspiration for much of New York's art production during the early 1970s but the way SoHo has come to serve as a yardstick for the transformation of urban areas through art. Since the sociologist Sharon Zukin wrote her influential account, *Loft Living*, in 1982 detailing how the artistic colonisation of SoHo's industrial lofts in the early 1970s ultimately became a valuable commodity in post-industrial New York, property developers and planners in cities from Montreal to Shanghai have proactively used the SoHo avant-garde 'aura' to popularise and legitimate spaces previously associated with manufacturing (Podmore, 1998; Kirby, 2002). Zukin (2001: 259) herself, writing in the accompanying book for *Century City* states how 'on the strength of New York's example, loft living has become a paradigm for cultural centres around the world'. It seems as if 'New York 1969–1974' lingers on as an idealised bohemia that can be readily reproduced, not just in New York itself, but in other cities sharing a similar stock of industrial built fabric and sufficient middle classes eager to distinguish a new place for themselves within the contemporary city.

Mumbai and Lower Parel would appear to possess these ingredients necessary for an imminent 'SoHo-isation'. Lower Parel contains a rich array of ornate industrial facades and cast-iron framed buildings, the earliest of which date, like SoHo's, from the 1850s. As well as containing suitable built fabric, Mumbai also has an expanding transnational middle class. India's liberalisation has increased the disposable income of a large segment of Mumbai's population; Karmali and Wagstyl (1994) estimate that salaries for its financial elites rose 300% in 1993–1994. Yet despite these factors, and the SoHo imaginaries that the Sakshi gallery and Charles Correa's report engender, Lower Parel's derelict mills are unlikely in the short term to be redeveloped on the SoHo model. This is clearly evidenced in the empty mill buildings still surrounding the Sakshi Gallery. As its owner, Geetha Mehra explains:

> My disappointment is that when I moved here to Shree Ram Mills I thought it would perhaps initiate this whole area … lots of retail outlets which would be somewhat high-end, it could be furnishings, home needs, auction houses, furniture, whatever. But none of that has happened, which I find rather disappointing.

Since the Sakshi opened in 1997, and despite several proposed schemes, no other major galleries have followed Sakshi's example of converting industrial space in Lower Parel. It would appear that the aspirations to equate Lower Parel with SoHo are presently misconceived.

This is primarily because Lower Parel, in contrast to 1960s SoHo, possesses a sizeable working-class residential population and bustling street life, which serves to inhibit any potential bohemian makeover. Despite a 1.5% decline in its population in the 1980s, Lower Parel retains many of the families that had been employed for several generations in the area's mills, most living in crowded, dilapidated tenements known as *chawls* and now earning a living from Mumbai's informal sector and often its criminal gangs. Furthermore, the area operates as 'an active political terrain' (Chandavarkar, 1998: 103). As the site of incipient Indian communism in the 1920s, major anti-British protest in the 1940s and militant trade unionism culminating in the protracted strike of 1982–1983, the area is an important symbol and setting for local and national political struggles. In the last ten years, mill redevelopments have been mired in controversy as stringent planning regulations protecting local workers have been regularly flouted (D'Monte, 2002). This strongly proletarian and politicised character of the locality means it is not easily conducive to reinterpretation as an artistic quarter.

In other cities, reinterpretations of traditionally proletarian areas have often been catalysed by an influx of cultural intermediaries; a 'critical infrastructure' of artists and other cultural producers that create new value for an area (O'Connor, 1998). This has very rarely occurred in Mumbai or Lower Parel. My initial queries as to whether any artists lived or worked in disused warehouse spaces were frequently met with bemused looks. I was told of only one contemporary artist who currently rents space in industrial premises, Sudarshan Shetty, who has a studio in a former iron vessel factory in Chinchpokli to the south-east of Lower Parel. On being asked why more artists have not followed his lead in relocating to an industrial space, he suggests, 'it is very expensive, the cost is too much, real estate is a huge problem'. Lower Parel's land prices quadrupled between 1988 and 1993 (Manchanda, 1993), and at the height of Mumbai's post-liberalisation real estate spiral in the mid-1990s, when rents in the business district of Nariman Point were the world's highest, the 5000 acres of mill-land were estimated to be worth $7.5 billion (D'Monte, 2001: 74). Unlike the attraction of cheap rents for artists in 1960s SoHo, space comes at a high premium in contemporary Mumbai.

Yet real estate in Lower Parel is still significantly cheaper than other parts of central Mumbai. Another reason why very few artists have exploited its spaces in a SoHo-esque fashion is the cultural parameters of art production in which they operate. As one of Mumbai's leading curators and art critics, Ranjit Hoskote, suggests:

> We live in a very conservative culture in terms of the way artists look at their careers, and how they develop. Artists don't step outside the mainstream. In the 50s, I think we missed the avant-garde bus because artists were too busy trying to get into the galleries. And in some ways we are the missing the bus again.

Despite the often conceptual nature of installation pieces in the Mumbai/Bombay section of *Century City*, the vast majority of the city's contemporary art is painting, influenced more by Impressionism than by Marcel Duchamp's ready-mades. This tendency to draw mainly from more traditional artistic notions of European modernism parallels and feeds the disinclination to forge new creative spaces in Mumbai's industrial districts. It is no coincidence that one of the only artists working in an industrial space, Sudarshan Shetty, is also one of the city's only large-scale sculptors.

This overall conservatism, in comparison with artistic practices in a city such as New York, is framed by deep polarisations within Mumbai society. Almost 68% of Greater Mumbai's population are homeless or housed in slums or dilapidated housing (Seabrook, 1996:49). Most people in Mumbai would understand 'loft living' as the perilously-built extra floor on a hutment or shack rather than a lifestyle that aesthetises industrial architecture. For Mumbai-based artists, the majority of whom are from middle-class or upper middle-class backgrounds, there is thus a certain reticence to relocate away from the city's perceived enclaves of modernity to an area such as Lower Parel. Occupying a redundant industrial space semi-legally, in the manner of the first SoHo artists, carries very different social connotations in a city where nearly everyone spends his life dreaming of proper accommodation (Appadurai, 2000). According to Geetha Mehra, owner of the Sakshi Gallery:

> It is very important where you live. I think Indians by and large have a lot of snob value, which I find doesn't exist in other parts of the world.

The vast majority of artists and galleries do not wish to be associated with an area viewed as down-market and poverty-stricken. Geetha Mehra's bold relocation to Lower Parel was probably assisted by how her gallery is a comparable newcomer to the social rigidities of Mumbai, having opened originally in Madras (now Chennai) in 1985 before shifting to Mumbai via Bangalore. For Sudarshan Shetty, his atypical move into the mill-lands was partly because, unusually for an artist in Mumbai, he was born in the mill area and spent the first ten years of his life in a chawl.

This vast gap between those who patronise contemporary art and the majority of Mumbai's residents means that contemporary art's profile and penetration across Mumbai society – and geography - is greatly limited. Most people, as Sandeep Pendse (1995) starkly illustrates, have little time and space for any cultural pursuits, let alone the transnationally-understood practices of contemporary art. This marginality of contemporary art extends to the political support it receives, as most politicians and municipal administrators in India and Mumbai have more pressing and parochial concerns and priorities. Whereas artists in SoHo benefited from an expansion of art school education in the 1960s and public financial support for major commissioning institutions, Mumbai's artistic infrastructure is minimal. This is why Sudarshan Shetty relies on overseas institutions for his livelihood:

> I don't have a market here at all – I have two buyers in Amsterdam and I've literally lived on them for a couple of years. And now I have a buyer in Japan and Korea. They come every year and they buy something.

Despite the recent growth of Mumbai's art scene, there are still comparatively few artists and collectors amongst the city's current population of fifteen million. This, together with an associated lack of state support and funding for contemporary art, means it is not surprising that Lower Parel has not undergone an artistic overhaul.

The upshot of this generally stubborn unreceptiveness of Lower Parel to art and artists – and vice versa – is that the area has not, so far, enjoyed the aesthetic revaluing of its industrial vernacular that SoHo underwent. Presently, there is no demand from Mumbai's middle-classes for conversions of industrial property, with preference given to new-build high-rises, complete with security guards and on-site leisure amenities. Incoming residents do not look to the potential artistic fashionability of Lower Parel but consider the area purely in economic terms. As one senior estate agent told me:

> I don't see that Bombay's mill-lands have come up with a very important image. What people are interested in Bombay is they understand the market, they understand business, so if they are getting some product at a rate cheaper than they normally secure, they will always go for that product in that particular place.

Lower Parel would seem to support neo-Marxist theories of gentrification, which prioritise the importance of capital exploiting devalorised central areas, rather than the significance of gentrifiers forging new inner-city lifestyles (e.g. Smith, 1987). For high-income groups, property in Lower Parel at the moment is conceptualised predominately as an investment rather than connected to new forms of cultural consumption.

Although SoHo (in the New York, 1969–1974, section) and Lower Parel (in the Bombay/Mumbai, 1992–2001, section) were featured in the same exhibition at the Tate Modern Gallery in 2001 and have been directly linked by artists, architects and journalists with experience of both areas, the urban contexts and consequences for art in each diverge considerably. This short essay has tried to open up some of the complexities and specificities of contemporary Mumbai. It has aimed to show how loft living as a lifestyle model and stimulus for transforming historic industrial districts cannot necessarily be transposed from its New York context, even though Mumbai shares with New York both a history of rapid deindustrialisation at its centre and a status as a major international commercial metropolis. Contemporary art in Mumbai operates and is produced within a different cultural, social and political framework and subsequently has a very different place in the city. This is often forgotten in the post-liberalisation zeal to project Mumbai as a globally sophisticated space; there is a tendency to ignore the ways contemporary art actually relates to the practices and imaginations of its citizens.

Secondly, this essay has tried to open out a consideration of the role of art in urban space beyond its usual setting within New York and, following the example of *Century City*, which also featured Rio de Janeiro and Lagos, beyond an overwhelming Eurocentric, Western bias. Although Sharon Zukin regularly comments on the diffusion and replication of loft living beyond the confines of New York, her own research on art districts is generally restricted to Manhattan and often directly or indirectly confers paradigmatic status for that city. An area such as SoHo should be seen more as a symbolic system of imagery that is spread between cities by transnational actors, particularly architects, master planners, designers and indeed academics. It is necessary to study how these actors discursively and historically construct understandings of the role of art in cities, exploring the concrete articulations that unfold in their attempts at the cultural production and contestation of place. For example, the initial creation of SoHo itself feeds off the imagery of Parisian ateliers in the early decades of the twentieth century.

Yet in a similar manner to the gallery attendants' occasional winding up and down of one of Atul Dodiya's three shutters, attempting to open up Mumbai's symbolic economy by investigating the area of Lower Parel, and the role of contemporary art, has also meant shutting down perspectives. Mumbai's infinite variety and contradictions defy any easy narrative and summary, and any attempt to explain the city will always result in missing viewpoints and stories. Comparisons and links could have been made with districts other than SoHo, other forms of cultural consumption such as shopping, fashion or restaurants could have been included, other areas such as Colaba (dubbed CoHo by one American art dealer) explored, other individuals interviewed and quoted. The focus here has been on Lower Parel because I was first introduced to Bombay/ Mumbai in a redundant industrial space – that of the former power station of the Tate Modern, which according to the editor of Art India, Sangita Jindal (2000) 'looks like some of the old mills in Lower Parel'. And the focus has been on art because of the successful, relevant and exciting way I felt the Mumbai art works on display at Century City managed to combine global themes with distinct local imaginaries. I was left with the impression that Atul Dodiya's shutters, produced in 2001 especially for the Tate, will also feature in an exhibition celebrating the twenty-first century.

Bibliography

Appadurai, A. (2000) Spectral housing and urban cleansing: Notes on millennial Mumbai. Public Culture. 12, pp.627-651.

Balaram, G. (1996) Parel's old mills can house a textile museum, says panel. Times of India, 13 October.

Balaram, G. (1998) A historic pocketborough is set to become a 'jewel of an art district'. Times of India, 16 August.

BMRDA (1995) Draft regional plan for Bombay Metropolitan Region 1996–2011 Bombay Metropolitan Region Development Authority.

Chandavarkar, R. (1998) Imperial power and popular politics. Class resistance and the state in India, c.1850-1950. Cambridge: Cambridge University Press.

D'Monte, D. (2001) Land and greed. Art News Magazine of India, vol VI, issue IV, pp.74-77.

D'Monte, D. (2002) Ripping the fabric: the decline of Mumbai and its mills. New Delhi: Oxford University Press.

Hoskote, R. (1998) Art gallery cuts swathe through mill area, holds promise of new SoHo. Times of India, 21 June.

Jindal, S. (2000) Editorial. The Art News Magazine of India, vol V, issue III, pp. 3.

Karmali, N. and Wagstyl, S. (1994) Financial reforms create a 'Wall Street' elite in India. Financial Times, 2 June, pp. 22.

Kirby, S. (2002) Collecting China. Wallpaper. October, pp.106-112.

Manchanda, U. (1993) A new lease of life for Bombay's mills. Economic Times, 7 November, pp.10.

Masselos, J. (1995) Postmodern Bombay: fractured discourses. In Watson, S. and Gibson, K. (eds.), Postmodern cities and spaces. Oxford: Blackwell, pp.199-215.

Nicholson, M. (1995) Survey of Maharashtra (1). Financial Times, 19 June, page I (supplement).

Ninan, E. (2000) That art-o-meter just keeps on rising. *The Times of India*, 17 February.

O'Connor, J. (1998) Popular culture, cultural intermediaries and urban regeneration. In Hall, T. and Hubbard, P. (eds.). *The entrepreneurial city: geographies of politics, regime and representations*. Chichester: John Wiley and Sons, pp. 225–239.

Paradkar, S. (1997) Parel: requiem or renaissance? *Indian Architect and Builder* January, pp. 26-29.

Patel, P. (1998) Slow Steps to Soho. *Indian Architect and Builder*, pp. 67-71.

Pendse, S. (1995) Toil, sweat and the city. In Patel, S. and Thorner, A. (eds.). *Bombay: metaphor for modern India*. New Delhi: Oxford University Press, pp. 3-25.

Podmore, J. (1998) (Re)Reading the 'loft living' habitus in Montreal's inner city. *International Journal of Urban and Regional Research* 22, pp. 283-302.

Seabrook, J. (1996) *In the cities of the South: scenes from a developing world*. London: Verso.

Simpson, C. (1981) *SoHo: the artist in the city*. Chicago: University of Chicago Press.

Smith, N. (1987) Gentrification and the rent-gap, *Annals of the Association of American Geographers* 77 (3), pp. 462-465.

Ty-Tomkins Seth, N. (1981) Art galleries. *Bombay City Magazine* 22 August - 6 September, pp. 113-117.

Zukin, S. (1982) *Loft living: culture and capital in urban change*. London: Johns Hopkins University Press.

Zukin, S. (2001) How to create a culture capital: reflections on urban markets and places. In Blazwich, I. (ed.) *Century city: art and culture in the modern metropolis*. London: Tate Publishing, pp. 258-264.

Notes

1   This essay draws from research and interviews carried out in Mumbai in February 2002 and between October 2002 and March 2003. These visits were made possible by ESRC award number R42200134230.

2   From 'Independent Interventions by Individulas, NGOs and Institutions' compiled by Mumbai's KRVIA architectural school especially for *Century City*.

Alastair Snow

Monuments and Monkey Puzzles;
Public Art in Bristol

Douglas Merritt's book *Sculpture in Bristol* published by the Redcliffe Press in 2002 outlines how sculpture in Bristol has been commissioned in different ways since 1736 as memorial, monument, architectural ornament, landscape feature and in the case of Andrew Smith's *Lollypop Be-bop* sited outside the Bristol Royal Hospital for Children, playfully eccentric, a dramatic, vivid, modern addition to the streetscape and very welcoming to anxious children arriving at the hospital for treatment.

Douglas refers to how the fine and noble art of patronage has changed – from public subscription to public art–with examples of corporate art and civic art that test and challenge different definitions of beauty and the changing thresholds of public taste.

In 1731 'a great number of gentlemen and other inhabitants' voted to subscribe to 'the memory of our Great and Glorious Deliverer the late King William III' and subscribed 'towards erecting in Queen Square a fine equestrian statue in brass' (Merritt, 2002). It is now grade I listed in a refurbished square.

There is a responsibility to care for distinguished, mature works of art but how best can new public art be commissioned in 2003? What is the status and priority for the arts in the public realm, for example as part of high quality urban design; and how can 'work' be generated as opposed to prescribed for artists? What agendas must the arts be linked with now to stimulate investment and patronage ? With a recent artwork by Damien Hirst marooned near Mars and the Multiple Store promoting *What is History* with two cast resin busts of Monica Lewinsky and Osama bin Laden, originally commissioned in 1998 as '*testimonies to the reality that an individual can become a player not only by reason and will but through sex and terror*[2] patronage has crossed a further frontier.

Prompted by the events in New York in September 2001 Michael Kimmelman wrote in the New York Times:

> *Centuries ago, when public art was commissioned by royalty, aristocrats and the church, official taste was synonymous with high art. Democracy and the modern era altered all that. Official art in a democracy requires consensus, an aesthetic common denominator. Modern art, however, is about one person's vision (the artist). The idea of consensus is antithetical to it. Its concerns are often entirely formal: line, colour, mass and weight (or conceptual). Memorial art, on the other hand, is therapeutic, redemptive and educational. These are different things. Modern artists also love ambiguity and irony. Monument builders do not.* 'The notion of a modern monument', Lewis Mumford wrote 60 years ago, 'is a contradiction in terms. If it is a monument, it is not modern and if it is modern, it cannot be a monument' (Kimmelman, 2002).

How can democracy and the modern era be interpreted? One way perhaps is to look at conference topics in the last decade of the previous century which considered key issues for cities in the twenty-first century.

These issues included: 'Shooting up the city – drugs and violence.' 'Who cares – is there a caring community?' Can we stop the rot – partnerships in the city? Profits and motifs – business and employment. Building the image – design and selling the city. Brussels or bust – is Europe the answer? Inclusion and exclusion: sub-groups and minority cultures; impact on the elderly, the young, children, disabled people, black and ethnic groups. Generating and sustaining the 24 hour economy. The 24 hour city – for or against? Relaxing the planning regime. Mixed use in residential areas. Night clubs – nuisance or economic generator? The Pink Pound – should gay culture be treated as a special case or just part of the mainstream leisure industry? Lighting – the way to safer streets.

Artists may sometimes refer to these issues in their work. One theme of the Aperto at the Venice Biennale in 1993 was 'Emergency' curated by Flash Art and described as:

> An up to date panorama of young artists who apply their linguistic experimentation to the problems of modern society and in particular to five emergencies: entropy, violence, survival, social emancipation and difference (Flash Art, 1993).

It was something of a surprise to link Flash Art with Sir John Harvey Jones who wrote

> Technology does not replace the role and contribution of the individual. The artist and we shall always need them, combine through the use of the whole range of human skills such extra elements as proportion, difference, originality and the ability to work with the grain or the particular, unique characteristics of the materials they work with. (Jones)

In the run-up to Year of the Artist in 2000 an a-n conference in Newcastle targeted new visual art and design graduates with a clear focus on the professional development needs of artists and designers at an early career stage. Anya Gallaccio opened the conference suggesting:

> You need a context for your work – make your own. Be wary of promises - don't take sweets from strangers.

John Darwell, photographer promoted:

> Don't let someone else's vision take over your own.

How can this vision be supported to enable artists to become more confident with their work and practice? 'New Sites – New Art' was the title of the first Baltic seminar held in Gateshead in 2000. Sune Nordgren suggested:

So much of contemporary art is produced outside artists studios on site. The question is how can the sites – in particular museums and galleries – support and stimulate new art and new artistic creation?

On exhibition at Baltic in 2002 was the work of the Portuguese artist Pedro Cabrita Reis who believes

> that in any art work what is to be perceived is that very particular, brief and silent moment when one experiences Intelligence, an absolute and total Intelligence through which everything comes together... Being a revelation of all our fears, Art neither changes life nor explains death. Such magnificent inability to provide a destiny makes Art different from science, religion and philosophy. As an attempt for meaning or sense, this might as well as be (why not?) a search for Beauty. I like to see my work as a part of this method of thinking.

One commentator of Pedro Cabrita Reis's work is Michael Tarantino who when considering the artist's 'search for beauty' refers to Primo Levi's 'The Periodic Table':

> There have been centuries in which 'beauty' was identified with adornment, the superimposed, the frills; but it is probable that they were deviant epochs and that the true beauty, in which every century recognises itself, is found in upright stones, ships' hulls, the blade of an axe, the wing of a plane.

Working in Bristol it is helpful to have a pragmatic understanding of the social and economic contrasts across the city, from the glamorous city centre to the poorer outer neighbourhoods.

> For those who pass it without entering, the city is one thing; It is another for those who are trapped by it and never leave. There is the city where you arrive for the first time; And there is another city which you leave never to return. (Calvino)

It can take time to acknowledge respective, cultural expectations in Bristol that influence and give a framework for the development of public art – to ensure a legible city – and involve all people living and possibly working in the city centre and outer neighbourhoods.

The bid from Bristol to become European City of Culture in 2008 attempted to address certain disparities picked up by Jeremy Isaacs, the chairman of the 2008 judging panel when he referred to Bristol as a

> divided city and the need to promote inter-activity between the posher and the poorer parts of the city.

Andrew Kelly, director of the 2008 team in Bristol has suggested that

the bid was not just about buildings but about people and participation.

The development of the public art programme in Bristol applies these two observations.

The Bristol Public Art Strategy places public art within the planning and development process; complementary to good urban and building design; integral within new development schemes; as part of social investment in new and refurbished housing, improvements to open public space, arts and health initiatives, towards creative and neighbourhood renewal.

The strategy acknowledges wide consultation with local people, artists, planners, architects, key service providers, arts venues and other organisations working together in the public realm. An enhanced Public Art Policy and revised statements within the Bristol Local Plan 2001–2011 aims to embed public art in key renewal projects to promote city and neighbourhood identity in the future. The strategy outlines how Bristol City Council intends to implement the Public Art Policy and gives guidance as to how to commission artworks of high quality. A new approach to public art is encouraged, integrated with the corporate priorities of Bristol City Council; multi-directorate in philosophy and application; and integral to education, housing, environment, transport, planning, social, health and cultural services. A new framework will enable wider public engagement in public art in both the city centre and outer neighbourhoods. This will build on the existing links with the planning and development control process and encourage on a voluntary basis the commission and provision of art and craftwork by public and private sector developers. Attention to the quality of urban design will encourage more work for artists and demonstrate and achieve new models of art in the public realm.

There is a meeting point between community regeneration objectives and the opportunities for aligned arts development. It gives opportunity for accessible, inclusive, outreach programmes to enable public engagement with the arts on the margins rather than in mainstream or more established locations. This is the context for arts development at a local level where collaborative relationships between artists and local people can provide a relevant framework and starting point to generate access and achievement in the arts for all people.

In 2004 four public art demonstration projects are being supported in Neighbourhood Renewal Priority Areas in Bristol: the St Paul's Learning and Family Centre in Ashley; the Wellspring (Healthy Living) Centre in Barton Hill; 'Spacemakers' in Hartcliffe; and the 'The Art of Well Being' project at Knowle West Health Park.

Good public art is sitespecific. It can help to define public space. The commission and design of public art should be informed by the associative qualities of a particular location as defined in respective development briefs.

It should be integral with urban design principles and expectations. The means to achieve public art should reflect planning guidance, corporate policies and delivery mechanisms to provide a consistent, coherent approach towards the regular commission of art of high quality in the public realm.

The location of two full-time public art officer posts within the Department of Environment, Transport and Leisure of Bristol City Council is designed to enable the planning authority to monitor planning applications and ensure that public art is integrated into major development proposals. It is advocated that public art is presented in the context of planning obligation, which under national planning guidance (PPG1) highlights aspects of design as a material consideration. Bristol City Council will profile and support the commissioning of public art through the Development Control process, respective development briefs, the use of planning conditions and Section 106 planning agreements.

Artists and makers, their individual practice, presence and creative output are important to the cultural infrastructure of a city. In fact, they make up a significant subsector of Bristol's burgeoning creative industries sector. Public art commissions can contribute by creating employment opportunities for artists, makers and fabricators who in turn utilise local industry, skills and resources. Other than by the purchase of artwork, investment in visual arts practice can be extended to specific commission and the involvement of artists in the design and use of the public realm. A distinction of Bristol City Council's public art programme is the opportunity it gives to artists interested in working to commission within architecture, transport and public realm information and identity projects, especially as part of the Bristol Legible City initiative.

Castle Park is apparently where Bristol began and is one of the city's most important archaeological sites. The History Trail covers a time span of a thousand years from the city's Saxon origins to the present day. In the 1980s this riverside area was in need of major refurbishment and a public art component was added to the landscape redevelopment plan. Commissioned artists collaborated with landscape architects, archaeologists, Bristol City Museum and Art Gallery and the local community, united by a strong sense of environmental commitment, an interest in Castle Park's history and new ideas for incorporating art in the landscape.

Commissioned artworks include: *Beside the Still Waters* by Peter Randall Page, who worked with Bristol City Council landscape architects using Kilkenny limestone, Pennant stone, horn beam hedge and pleached lime trees; *Drinking Fountain* in bronze by Kate Malone; *Herb Garden Railing* by Alan Evans; and park benches in oak and steel by Alan Tilbury.

In 2000 as part of Year of the Artist, Bristol City Council commissioned artist Helen Schell to produce a flowering artwork for Castle Park with 20,000 tulip and daffodil bulbs planted in November. The project complemented Annie Lovejoy's Year of the Artist residency with the Parks Service to create the Purdown Man, an ecological artwork made up of 5,000 ox-eye daisies.

> I wanted to create a work that celebrated the preservation of an intriguing landscape easily accessible via public rights of way from the inner city. The familiar pedestrian symbol is

environmentally recreated in urban parkland and draws on the history of figurative icons in the landscape.

Dedicated on 16 March 1999, the **Pero Footbridge** across St Augustine's Reach links Narrow Quay and Queen's Square with a new Millennium Square across the water. The bridge is named after Pero, a slave who worked on the Caribbean sugar plantation of the leading eighteenth century Bristol merchant John Pinney. It was achieved in a design collaboration between artist Eillis O'Connell and engineers Ove Arup, commissioned by the JT Group as part of their waterfront development in 1998.

@t Bristol is a major regeneration Millennium project and has provided the city with a significant new leisure and recreational resource with a unique interface between science, technology, wildlife, the environment and public art. Commissions include:

Aquarena by William Pye with two prism-shaped monoliths in mirror-polished stainless steel, a shimmering wall of water and water terraces. *WET* was a film/dance collaboration by Rachel Bowen (film) and Lisa Thomas (choreography) centred on William Pye's sculpture and presented as part of Dance Live Bristol in September 2002. *Zenith* by David Ward features 52 helicopter lights and is inspired by an analemma – the line traced by the sun recorded at noon over the course of a year as used in the past by navigators, explorers and astronomers. *Small Worlds* by Simon Thomas, is a four metre high abstract sculpture to commemmorate the work of physicist Paul Dirac and his discovery of anti-matter. A life-size sculpture by Graham Ibbeson of Bristol-born actor Cary Grant was sited in Millennium Square in 2001.

Douglas Merritt's book *Sculpture in Bristol* honours and highlights the touchstones of memory and achievement to be found in the streets of Bristol. Memorial art enhances the everyday with pointers to the past. It can give cause for reflection, entertain and stimulate broad judgement and awareness. It can also stand as testament to the role of artists in creating artworks, perhaps in less traditional ways, to add renewed status, character and dynamic quality to a European Centre of Culture.

Sean Griffiths from Fashion, Architecture and Taste (FAT) is the lead artist for **Bristol Legible City** and is appointed to contribute at a strategic level to the development of the role of artists within the project and to carry out specific commissions.

High Life, Walkie Talkie, Edible Playscape and *Bristol Bridge* are four commissions on the pedestrian route that links the city centre's three regeneration areas – Harbourside, Temple and Broadmead. The aim of these commissions is to investigate the identity of sites on the route with artworks that convey additional layers of meaning. *High Life* consists of eight artworks by artists Antoni and Alison, FAT, Kathleen Herbert, Luke Jerram, John Pym, Julian Opie, Seamus Staunton and Elizabeth Wright. The artworks, which each contain a bird box, are installed within the trees of Queen Square and were created in response to the ecology, history, design and use of the square. *Walkie-Talkie* by visual artist Colin Pearce and poet Ralph Hoyte, was a temporarily installed 600 metre line of pavement text the appearance of which drew on the placement, colour and font of the Bristol Legible City pedestrian signage system. The text conveyed an alternative way of understanding the city by representing a mixture of voices that combined everyday, chatty conversation with contemporary poetry and local historical facts and references. *Edible Playscape* by Nils Norman and commissioned in partnership with the Arnolfini took the form of leaflets and posters that proposed the conversion of a city centre roundabout into a community allotment. FAT was commissioned to propose enhancements to *Bristol Bridge*, which is located at one of the city's most important historical sites and is critical to vehicle and pedestrian movement in the city centre. The proposals included the enhancement of the bridge's balustrade, paving and lighting.

At present other projects are being developed as part of Bristol Legible City. These include *Blaise* and *City-gates*, which are working titles of projects that will consist of the presentation of a series of permanent or temporary artistic interventions that contribute to the visitor's experience of Blaise Castle Estate and the contemporary significance of the city's medieval walls and gateways.

The Bristol Legible City public art programme is also supporting the work of **Art and Power,** which is a membership-led organisation of disabled artists who use a variety of art forms to inform, challenge and inspire. Many of Art and Power's members have experienced life in a range of institutions and have often been labelled, separated and marginalised from public life. Having started out in a day centre for adults with learning difficulties, the group is now celebrating hard-won status as a key arts provider to the City of Bristol. It is the group's ambition to play a key role in developing a more inclusive and creative city.

One way the group meets this commitment is through the access to the arts transport research project. The aim of the project is to improve access to the city's arts venues for disabled people by improving the user's understanding and experience of the city's public transport network. Informed by the work of Bristol Legible City, projects are being developed that aim to improve the quality of service disabled people receive from bus operators and to improve the design and identity of buses, bus stops, timetables and other resources that are important when navigating the city. The projects have a wide-ranging, partnership approach and illustrate how the arts can be an effective tool for delivering social change

Harbourside, Broadmead and Temple are the three main regeneration areas in the city centre where major development is planned. New shopping and leisure facilities, office accommodation, housing, roads, bridges, streets and open public spaces will have an enormous impact on the physical appearance and the economic and social vitality of the city centre.

On **Harbourside,** Crest Nicholson is beginning to develop Cannon's Marsh, which is currently one of the largest mixed-use development schemes in Europe. Elsewhere, other developers – for example, Crosby Homes, Deely Freed and London Paris – are also developing schemes that will capture the unique character of respective Harbourside locations.

Broadmead is Bristol's main retail area, which the Bristol Alliance is proposing to expand by building a significant amount of new retail space. The development will be made possible by realigning a section of the city's inner ring road.

At **Temple** the Temple Quay core site, which has provided much needed city centre office accommodation, has been completed and plans are now being implemented by the South West Regional Development Agency and the developer Castlemore to build a mixed-use development on the Quay's north shore.

The developers responsible for implementing these schemes and in other, smaller developments elsewhere in the city centre have been encouraged by the Council to recognise the benefits of commissioning artists. There is an acceptance that artists have an important role in enhancing the quality of the built environment by realising commissions that signify the identity of the development and the city; to encourage exploration of the city during the day and at night; to enable way finding; to connect new developments to existing neighbourhoods and to encourage the choice of sustainable modes of transport. Artists such as Nayan Kulkarni, John Aitken, John Packer, Julian Coode, Peter Freeman and Martin Richman are currently working with developers.

Arnolfini is one of Europe's leading centres for the contemporary art with a national and international reputation for presenting new and innovative work in the visual arts, dance, performance, film and live art. *Still Ringing* was a combined artwork for unaccompanied voice, dance and handbells presented in 1997 at the Lead Works in Bristol. *Still Running*, produced by hAb in 1999 from an original idea by Municipal Corporations, used video, glass, octophonic sound and live performance in a multi-sensory digital work presented in a multi-storey car park. *PARA-CITIES: Models for Public Spaces* was an exhibion of recent architectural proposals installed in an environment at Arnolfini in 2001 designed by Vito Acconci and the Acconci Studio. The artist Susanna Heron is working with the Design Team and architect Robin Snell Associates to advise Arnolfini's planned development phase 2002–2005. Four *Escaped Animals* road signs devised by Julian Opie were sited outside Arnolfini to symbolically point the way to the Baltic Centre for Contemporary Art, which opened in Gateshead in July 2002.

Spike Island combines artists' studio provision with an artistic programme of exhibitions and events. Housed in the landmark Brooke Bond building, previously a tea-packing factory, it contains over seventy studios, an expansive central exhibition space, visiting artists' residency studios, workshop facilities and commercial tenants.

Tania Abadjieva was Spike Island Visiting Arts Fellow in 2001 and with the Bristol Arrow Bowling Club and the City and County of Bristol Bowls Club created an installation entitled 'Drawing Wood'.

> Drawing Wood evolves directly from Abadjieva's observations of England and the experience of a game of lawn bowls. She has taken this slice of Englishness and transported it into the gallery space at Spike Island. Extracting themes, distilling atmosphere, inserting them into an alternative environment, she has constructed a participatory event on a grand scale.

Jamaica Street Studios are home to over forty of Bristol's most contemporary artists. Spread over four floors in a building with a rich history dating back to the turn of the century, the studios are used to produce work ranging from video and installation to painting and sculpture. **Centrespace,** formerly Bristol Craft Centre, provides studio workspace to over twenty artists, designers and makers. The **Epstein Building** in Mivart Street provides studios for artists, photographers, performers and musicians. Studio workspace for artists and makers is also available at the **Robinson Building** in Bedminster. **Front Room** was the lower Totterdown art trail held in November 2001 and 2002 with fine art and craftwork exhibited by twenty artists in ten houses. The **North Bristol Visual Artists Group** held a similar event in seven houses and Café Unlimited in November 2002. Artists and makers in Southville, Bedminster and Windmill Hill were invited to be part of the **Southville Arts Trail** around artists' workshops and studios held in June 2003.

In the autumn 2000 the Independent Artists Network (IAN) presented **Workplace,** a multi-disciplinary arts event which showcased emerging and established artists in Bristol and the south-west region.

> For many artists the opportunity to show new work to a local audience is often limited to the formality of the conventional gallery/performance space. Workplace enabled more than 100 artists to present their work in a variety of empty or disused council buildings and spaces. These industrial, commercial and historic sites provided a rare opportunity to discover contemporary art and performance in disregarded or unfamiliar areas of the city. (Indepedent).

In 2003 IAN presented **dialogue** with artists from Bristol, Hanover and Porto who were commissioned to present temporary artworks and interventions created in response to the city's floating harbour, which included a silent film sequence of a blind accordion player in Opporto by Gabriela Vaz, multi-lingual, conversing cranes by Natalie Deseke and hidden glimpses of performance artist Eve Dent.

There are clear links between the quality of the environment, good design and good health. **Bristol Royal Hospital for Children** re-opened in 2001 in a new building with artworks commissioned by artists including Ray Smith, who worked as lead artist with the interior design team; glass artist, Catrin Jones; Roger Michell, who completed a series of ceramic panels for the hydrotherapy pool; Walter Jack, who made seating and screen forms; a poet-in-residence, Bertel Martine; a DVD light box by Carolyn Black; and an eighteen metre high interactive sculpture with fibre optics by Andrew Smith sited outside the main entrance entitled Lollypop Be-bop.

The Dorothy Hodgkin Building (DHB) will be a landmark construction in the centre of Bristol to provide dedicated medical research laboratories for the University of Bristol Research Centre for Neuroendocrinology (URCN) from 2003. In gaining planning permission, the University was encouraged to incorporate an artwork within the building commissioned from Anna Heinrich and Leon Palmer. The project is funded by the University of Bristol, The Wellcome Trust and Arts Council England.

The URCN has an international standing in research into the interaction between the brain and circulating hormones under conditions of disease and stress.

In Bristol, public art aims to empower and involve local communities in creative renewal and to demonstrate new links between arts and health.

Knowle West Health Park is a new national flagship project which promotes new approaches to addressing ill health. *The Art of Well Being* celebrates a new creative partnership, with Michael Pinsky as lead artist for the public art programme with Benedict Phillips and Elpida Hadzi-Vasileva, and Zoe Walker and Neil Bromwich as media/digital artists in residence. A windows screening commission for the Renal Dialysis Unit on site at the Health Park has been awarded to the artist Deborah Jones.

Community at Heart is the organisation set up to manage the Bristol New Deal for Communities programme in Barton Hill, Lawrence Hill, Redfield and the Dings. By the end of 2003, a new **Healthy Living Centre** will open in **Barton Hill**. From the outset, there has been enthusiasm from local residents 'that there should be art – both inside and out'. Subsequently, a public art project has been devised with lead artist Marion Brandis appointed at an early stage to work closely with the architects and members of the project groups and identify a series of art commissions integral to the building, with glass by Anne Smythe, metal gates by Julian Coode, a wooden staircase surround and reception desk by Walter Jack; internal signage by Lucy Casson, paving designs for the reception and courtyard areas by Marion Brandis

In the summer 2002, Gloria Ojulari Sule worked as artist researcher with the Building Design Team to advise the planning and development of **St Paul's Learning and Family Centre**. She was commissioned to research preliminery ideas and outline design proposals for artworks, creative workshop facilities and exhibition spaces. These proposals were informed by project research and consultation with local people and community organisations associated with the planning of the new centre. She joined discussions of the Building Design Team and advised best approaches and opportunities for incorporating the arts and arts facilities as an integral part of the building and also within a developing programme of activity in the centre. Subsequently three artists, Chris Trow, Barbara Disney and Valda Jackson, were commissioned to make first stage design proposals for glass, mosaic and mural works supported by an art commissions programme consultant.

Spacemakers is a design project for young people aged between thirteen and fifteen living in the area surrounding the Hartcliffe Community Campus in south Bristol. The project promotes the effective and sustained involvement of young people in decisions affecting changes to the environment in Hartcliffe. A training arts and design programme with an emphasis on active learning will enable a group of young people to develop ideas with artists and landscape designers and help shape respective visions for the area. The project will develop the confidence and skills of young people and enable them to creatively participate in decisions affecting the rebuilding of their own spaces and wider environments. They will have access into the processes of architects, designers, artists and planners who both envision and create public spaces. A programme of capacity-building activities includes a three day residential training course at Trafford Hall, the home of the National Tenants Resource Centre, design research trips to see examples of high quality design in the built environment, an integral arts co-ordination programme including an idea to use SMS text messaging to foster a more appropriate style of information exchange between young people; project documentation with the Knowle West Media Project; and a series of artist residencies with Cleo Broda and Kathrin Bohm to establish a connection between Spacemakers and members of the wider community.

Major capital development of the **Colston Hall** will offer opportunity for artists to become part of the design process identified via a lead artist as an appointed member of the Colston Hall Design Team. Bristol City Council is committed to the practical involvement of artists in all aspects of the project and anticipate a programme of commissions of at least £200,000 as an integrated part of the design of the building. Michael Brennand-Wood has been appointed lead artist to work with architects Levitt Bernstein Associates, the Project Design Team and artist Richard Layzell.

New policy will define a structured approach and give a framework to enable public engagement in public art in the city centre and outer neighbourhoods. It will continue to be linked with the planning and development control process and encourage on a voluntary basis the commission and provision of art and craftwork by public and private sector developers. The Bristol Public Art Strategy aims simply to promote design quality and work for artists, to demonstrate and achieve new models and quality thresholds and raised expectations for art in the public realm; while mindful of the view that an artist is not a service organisation expected to come up with cheerful rescue plans for deprived areas. Moreover, it advocates the contribution of artists towards the achievement of shared development objectives of different agencies working together to influence positive change. The combination of local people and professional advisers from arts, architecture, landscape, planning and economic agencies aim to give foundation for successful project development in the future. The arts can offer a means to people to become more directly involved in local issues and major development opportunities that affect an area in which people live. Local people should contribute and be part of a process of change and renewal, without raising unnecessary or false expectation, promoted

> with those individuals, organisations and partnerships that make policy work on the ground – the police, street cleaners, neighbourhood and street wardens, community leaders, businesses, **artists,** contractors and local government (ODPM).

A key objective of the Bristol Public Art Strategy is to promote the value of research and consultation as an integral element within public art projects. It echoes a similar priority of the Neighbourhood Arts Strategy to generate a greater sense of ownership and public involvement in regeneration and change. Local development frameworks aim to promote greater community engagement with the planning process to seek

> direct participation from local people in shaping the future of their communities (Planning).

Artists can also work very effectively with local people and groups. They can enhance a 'sense of place' by helping people to articulate, in many different ways, the perception and experience of their environment (Arts Council England).

By 2008 an enhanced economy of the creative industries in Bristol will have recognised the respective professional development needs of artists and generated high quality commissioned work in the city centre and outer neighbourhoods. Bristol Legible City will have uncovered further layers of information and meaning to places and routes on Harbourside, in Broadmead, Redcliffe and Temple. Artist interventions will have been presented along major pedestrian and transport routes, public open spaces and development sites which together with an annual programme of permanent works and temporary interventions by local, regional, national and international artists, will assist in making Bristol a modern, European, safe and legible city.

Bibliography

Calvino, I. The Invisible City.

Exhibition catalogue. Baltic 2000.

Flash Art. (1993) 'Emergency' catalogue, Venice Biennale.

Hunter, K. What is History? Commissioned by The Multiple Store.

Independent Artists Network. Bristol.

Jones, Sir John Harvey Jones. Making it Happen.

Merritt, D. (2002) *Sculpture in Bristol*. Redcliffe Press.

Office of the Deputy Prime Minister (OPDM). (2002) Living Places, Cleaner, Safer, Greener. October.

Planning Green Paper Delivering a fundamental change.

Notes

1   Michael Kimmelman, *New York Times*, reprinted in *The Guardian*, 17 January 2002.

2   Anya Gallaccio, Fast Forward conference, a-n, 2000.

3   John Darwell, Fast Forward conference, a-n, 2000.

4   Sune Nordgren, 'New Sites – New Art', Baltic 2000.

5   Pedro Cabrita Reis, Exhibition catalogue, Baltic 2000.

6   Michael Tarantino, Exhibition catalogue, Baltic 2000.

7   Jeremy Isaacs, Chairman, 2008 Judging Panel, speaking on BBC Radio 4.

8   Andrew Kelly, Director, 2008 Judging Panel, speaking on BBC Radio 4.

9   Annie Lovejoy, commissioned artist.

10   Sally Shaw, Spike Island.

Friedrich von Borries and Matthias Böttger

BürgerMeister: New Tactics for Shrinking Cities

Introduction

Imagine a city shrinking. Instead of growing, the city becomes smaller every day. Many citizens leave the city, none move in. Flats stay vacant. Schools and kindergartens have to close. The young and active move away, seeking work in more prosperous regions. The population shrinks and ages.

This city is no fiction, it is reality. The process of shrinking has become a common trend in the cities in eastern Germany – for example, the population of Halle/Halle-Neustadt in 1989 was 329,000 inhabitants and in 2003 239,000, with an estimated population in 2010 of between 200,000 and 208,000. *The entity known as the European City is in a state of dissolution.* There are three main explanations for this development:

1. Exodus

12 years after reunification, the effort to transform the Fordist, industry-based economy of the GDR to a post-Fordist, service-based economy has failed. Helmut Kohl's promise of a 'blühende Landschaften' (blooming land) has not come true. Instead, the opposite seems to dominate: an unemployment rate of 20% and no hope for a change in the near future. The well educated and highly motivated young form a track to the West, looking for work. This 'brain drain' worsens the situation. Interestingly, the possible demographic and economical influences of the extension of the EU towards the East have not yet been fully explored in the current debate on shrinking cities.

2. Sprawl

The city in the GDR was characterized by bipolarity: old city centres contrasted the 'Plattenbauten', prefabricated high-rise apartment buildings. The latter, officially propagated as a socialist project, were well equipped, so that most people preferred them over nineteenth century buildings, which were less cared for and never refurbished. Today, the suburban house with a garden and a car-port are the dream of the East Germans and not lofts and belle-etages. The suburban sprawl is the new alternative to the historical centre.

3. Ageing

Based on demographic tendencies, Germany's population turns ever older and thus shrinks – as long as the low rate of reproduction is not balanced out by immigration (Germany's population in 2000 was 82 million; in 2050 without immigration it wil be between 52 and 55 million). In East Germany this effect is intensified by the emigration of the younger generation at the beginning of their working life.

Money Makes the World Go Round

Following the belief that money can buy everything, or at least change most things, the Federal Government, the state administration and the local authorities launched a gigantic programme called 'Stadt Umbau Ost' (city redesign East) with public funding of nearly 2.7 billion euros. The main focus of this revitalization project of the city centres was an attempt to save the European city characterised as 'nice', 'cosy' and 'picturesque'. There is eager activity: façades are redecorated, streets are paved anew with cobblestones, and empty builidings, especially the old East German high-rise apartment houses, are torn down.

Even innovative strategies like de-densification, perforation und renaturalisation are expensive attempts to find a new spatial organisation for shrinking regions through building or de-building. The essential question is: *Are other, more immaterial forms of intervention possible and feasible?*

Goodbye Master Plan – Hello *Raumtaktik*

Shrinking is often described as a problem of building space, which can be solved, following the traditions of town planning, with building activity – taking down and demolishing, as building is seen in its negative form. For the town planner, it is foremost a shift away from the paradigm of growth. The growth based discipline of town planning cannot address the phenomenon of shrinking. By focusing on building or rather 'un-building', one tends to forget that shrinking is as much a cultural as a psychological problem. The spatial phenomenon of the not controllable, unforeseen and unforeseeable implosion of a neighbourhood and its obvious degradation are only symptoms of a psychological process. In place of the master plan, with its focus on building and its long term approach, we put forward a more flexible, more reactive method of intervention: the *Raumtaktik* (spatial tactic).

Raumtaktik as Urban Mental Health Care

The urgency of tactical interventions in the psychological and social structure of the city becomes very clear in the case of shrinking cities. Vacant apartments and deteriorated façades are only superficial symptoms. The real problems are a lack of motivation, hopelessness and sadness – psychological conditions.

The complex process of socio-cultural transformation in shrinking cities and regions longs for a new form of spatial intervention. These interventions have to affect the psychological condition of the people living there and not necessarily the built environment. It is crucial to intervene directly in these 'mental maps', and to start a new form of spatial communication. This is because even the most intelligent therapies are bound to fail if the patients do not like them and do not make them their own and strengthen their effect.

In shrinking cities, the *Raumtaktiker* (spatial tactician) works as an urban therapist. He/she tries to open up new perspectives to the uneasy population, spreading energy and starting new activities. The *Raumtaktiker* is not to design new spatial configurations but to start and guide new processes and activities: the goal is to design new spheres of thinking, new spaces for possibilities and activities.

The *Raumtaktiker* pursues – symbolically speaking – urban mental health care.

In a different context, the *Raumtaktiker* might use completely different tactics for different tasks.

Let's Play *BürgerMeister*

Such a tactical intervention could be a board game, a game which is not proposed as an answer nor as tool for planning but as a new form of therapy.

A game as tactic intervention has to be a real game. Strategic role plays are often used in city planning as a means of participation; they are used to integrate the 'non-specialist' in the process of planning. These role plays are highly educational, often including an element of fun.

A game as a tactical instrument to activate has first to be, as paradoxical as it may sound, a game, a game creating a lot of fun, which equals engagement. One has to laugh, has to enjoy winning and to hate losing.

BürgerMeister is a strategic board game for 3 to 4 players. The goal is to stay mayor for as long as possible. Strategy cards used to deal with the process of shrinking and to keep the citizens happy and content. Event cards provide unforeseeable incidents which represent the continuous change of social and economic circumstances, to which every player has to relate.

By this process, each player gets to know the development possibilities of his city within a competitive situation.

Typical of a strategy game, at some point the players start to invent their own rules. The players begin to improve the game, adapt it to their personal circumstances. At this moment the players of *BürgerMeister* stop 'playing' and start to develop their home town. The board games becomes the city, the players active.

The aim of *BürgerMeister* is not the game itself, it is the city. *BürgerMeister* is a tool to start a process of activity and communication, necessary in shrinking cities. Otherwise the citizens cannot take part in the ongoing process of the city's transformation. *Play your city.*

For further information, see: **www.raumtaktik.de**

Chapter 1: Sangerhausen: A Case for the RAUMTAKTIKER...

2004

Silke, Ronny and Doreen live in Sangerhausen. Silke, 36 years old, is a solitary mother, retail assistent, Ronny, 29, is an unemployed mechanic and Doreen, 22, is looking for an internship ...

Chapter 2: The RAUMTAKTIKER arrives at Sangerhausen ...

Three Sangerhauseners are watching TV, when suddenly the doorbell rings - the **RAUMTAKTIKER** with his Tool-Kit appears at their door: Would you like to join me in ...

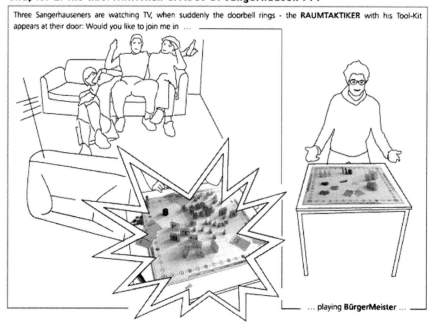

... playing **BürgerMeister** ...

Chapter 3: Preparing the GAME

BürgerMeister is a strategic board-game for 3-4 players. The goal is to stay mayor as long as possible by providing circumstances where the citizens are happy and content which is a good guarantee for success at the next election. Also content citizen tend not to move away. To keep it interesting carefully outlined strategies are sometimes proven wrong by unexpected incidents. And, as an extra: The city shrinks constantly with 100 citizens per player moving away per year.

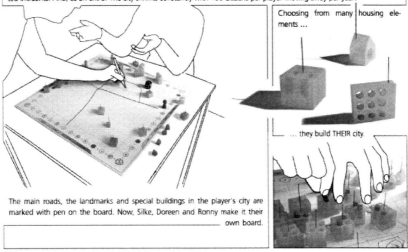

Choosing from many housing elements ...

... they build THEIR city.

The main roads, the landmarks and special buildings in the player's city are marked with pen on the board. Now, Silke, Doreen and Ronny make it their own board.

Chapter 4: Pearls of Content

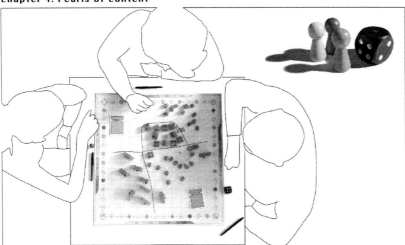

Buildings in good shape with a nice environment are marked with pearls of content. Buildings with many pearls and citizens living there are a sign for a comfortable and nice area.

The players discuss the shape of the board, thus drawing an abstract image of their environment, their own town. Agreeing on a common abstract image of their town, the game starts the second phase ...

Chapter 5: A complex move

Doreen throws a 3 and moves three steps forward. She plays a strategy card allowing her to set up a Pick-It-Yourself plantation of strawberries.
It costs 16 cents. The new plantation is marked with a pen on the board.
The plantation changes its surroundings, making it more livable. Doreen places five new pearls of content on houses of her choice.

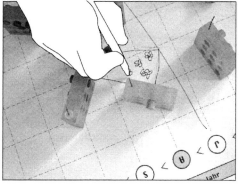

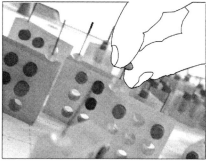

Now it is Ronny's turn ...

Chapter 6: New events, surprises occur, what counts in the end ...

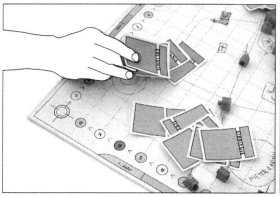

Whenever a player moves to a field claiming "event," he has to draw a card announcing a new event. Events either apply to only or to all the players. Carefully developed strategies - like in real life - are sometimes strengthened by these unforeseeable events, sometimes proven completely wrong.
The events try to simulate the complexity of a real town and enhance the game-play. After a while, they start to write down their own events and strategies on new cards ... Who keeps most citizens happy and in town, wins the game!

100 red citizens,
no pearls
= -100 points

100 red citizens,
two pearls
= +200 points

200 red citizens,
two pearls
= +400 points

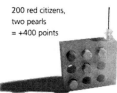

Chapter 7: After the GAME is before the CITY ...

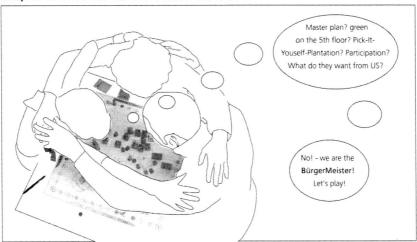

After several hours of playing the three have tested many different configurations of a new city. But in which city do they want to live? In a dense city, where you can walk to most places, to restaurants and bars? Or in a city of single houses, where everybody has a car and a garden? Or in landscape of high rises, which are renovated individually, allowing many new things to develop - an allotment garden and art galleries, playgrounds and workshops, plantations and forests - everything we can dream of? Or is the secret of a city somewhere else? ...

Chapter 8: The game GOES REAL !

There is no temporary use without temporary users - or sustainable changes in a shrinking city are not based on build intervention, but on the ACTIVATION of existing potentials and desires. BürgerMeister confronts the players with different strategies of productive shrinking and transformation, to start a process shrinking cities heavily rely on: CREATIVITY, IDENTIFICATION and ENGAGEMENT!

... and the RAUMTAKTIKER moves on ...

and Doreen is taking care for the Pluck-It-Yourself plantation and is rewarded for turning worthless public ground into a green and happy place.

Chapter 9: The RAUMTAKTIKER moves on ...

The RAUMTAKTIKER leaves Sangerhausen. His job is done. He has activated. With the game, he started a process. New initiatives have been formed and the first small projects came to life. He did not leave any written concept or plan to Sangerhausen, but a whole new mentality – *the will to do*. The game BürgerMeister is only a tool in this process; a tool to empower the citizens to be part of the game in their city, in their lives.

2024: Game Over for masterplans. The paradigm of planning has been abandoned. The RAUMTAKTIKER does not design or plan for any ideal goal, but starts a series of dialogs and processes. The RAUMTAKTIKER does not develop the big blueprint, but pictures dreams of a new everyday life. He looks up, there are many regions and towns anticipating his help. Let's play ...

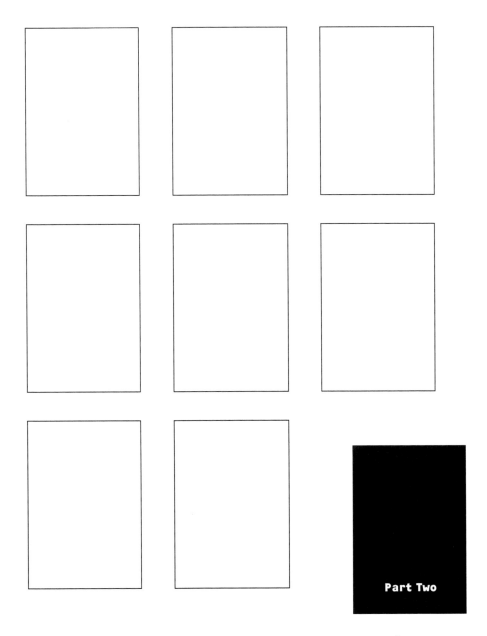

Part Two

Projects

Ben Campkin

Urban Image and Legibility in King's Cross, London[1]

...an area of the city which is designated an anomaly (i.e. which does not readily fit in one category or another), and unfitting to the desired urban order, not only is designated dirty, but literally begins to acquire dirt and collect things-out-of-place — the material symptoms of the thing we call urban neglect (Shonfield, 2000: 159).

Currently undergoing a rapid and intense period development and physical transformation, King's Cross, London, presents a timely and appropriate subject as the focus of questions of urban image, identity and legibility in the tenty-first century city. Based on research into urban regeneration in King's Cross, this paper explores some recent approaches to the representation and identification of the area. It is intended to raise questions of city image and identity relevant to contemporary regeneration within a broad cultural and historical context. The redevelopment and regeneration plans for the area are briefly introduced, together with some of the problems frequently ascribed to it. These are set within the context of the history of King's Cross and the 'popular' representation and construction of its image. Three recent projects are then elaborated as case studies that initiate a discussion of the legibility of the area, with Lynch's discussion of the concept in mind.[2] Firstly, the design of the British Library will be examined in terms of the notions of legibility and the architectural response to the area which it embodies. Secondly, the Almeida at King's Cross, a small-scale, low budget architectural urban regeneration project involving the conversion of a disued garage to a temporary theatre will be considered for the alternative approach to the identity of the area that it suggests. Finally, notions of legibility and the city will be examined as they are presented in the work of artist and King's Cross resident Richard Wentworth, whose recent project with Artangel, *An Area of Outstanding Unnatural Beauty* (2002) was based in a vacant plumbing warehouse in King's Cross.

Through an installation and series of talks, walks and games, *An Area of Outstanding Unnatural Beauty* challenged the popular perception of the area through a project which encouraged interaction with the urban environment, seeking to address the construction of the image of King's Cross and provoke questions regarding its present and possible future states.

Constructing an 'Illegible' Environment?

Since its development in the eighteenth and nineteenth centuries, the area has frequently been represented as dirty and undesirable and has been subject to numerous projects of 'improvement' and re-identification. This paper will therefore focus on mappings of King's Cross through perceived 'dirt' and legibility through design as a defence against perceived dirt and disorder. The imminent large-scale change associated with the development of the Channel Tunnel Rail Link, in formal terms comparable to the disruption brought about by the establishment of the railways and the construction of the St Pancras and King's Cross railway termini in the mid-nineteenth century, makes a consideration of the legibility of the past and future of the area timely. Contemporary attempts to re-brand the area through the subtle manipulation of architectural and visual detail will be examined in the context of its cultural and historical development.

In one sense King's Cross enjoys an almost unrivalled monumental architectural 'legibility' through numerous listed Victorian buildings that would be termed landmarks in Lynch's influential classificatory system, developed as a means of understanding the 'image' of the city. Until recently, the mid- to late-nineteenth century gasholders behind the two stations punctuated the landscape providing one of the most recognizable and evocative (if strange) images available in the city as a whole. A carcass of industrial London, the cityscape behind St Pancras and King's Cross stations became a point from which romanticisation of the industrial past was possible. Indeed, the proliferation of Victorian building stock has made the area a popular location for period films, as well as a fantasy setting for pop music videos and nighttime destination for clubbers. From the northern-most position of the railway lands behind King's Cross and St. Pancras stations looking south, the rest of London seems to have a peculiar legibility – this is surely one of the most expansive and dramatic urban panoramas available within central London. From another viewpoint, however, the King's Cross Railway Lands have been 'read' as an absence, or as 'derelict and degraded property which unquestionably needs renewal.' [3]

Most of the gasholders have recently been dismantled while their fate is decided, temporarily erased from the cityscape, probably to be reintroduced at a later stage in the development, perhaps being used to evoke nostalgia for a 'King's Cross' past (or imagined). This painstaking act of taking apart the gasholders piece by piece can be viewed as a metaphor for contemporary attempts to rename, rebrand and change the image of King's Cross. This, the largest brownfield development site in the UK, is an area currently undergoing rapid and large-scale physical transformation, with the Channel Tunnel Rail Link (CTRL) as the principal trigger. It is hoped that the development around the CTRL, designated 'King's Cross Central' by the landowners and developers, will bring much wider change to the area, so that by 2020 the fabric of this part of London will have undergone dramatic transformation and will look, feel, smell and sound like an entirely different place, projecting an entirely different city image. It is anticipated, of course, that this new image will in turn affect associated social and economic adjustment.

Fixing a Moving Target

In the discourse around the proposals for the area the main developers, Argent St. George, have initiated a discussion of 'principles', 'parameters', and 'frameworks', defining the future of the area through notions of clarity, structure and legibility. However, these notions, and the processes through which decisions have been and are being made, are frequently ambiguous and open to question. The three examples I will go on to elaborate will demonstrate at different architectural and urban scales that, in relationship to place and identity, the notion of legibility in design tends towards an abstraction, disengaged from the everyday reality of the lives of city users.

The need to change and improve King's Cross, to regenerate the area, has been taken as given for quite some time. Despite its inner city location, intensive use and importance to London's transport networks, the area has suffered through a lack of investment since the cessation of industrial activity associated with the railway. However, though there might be unanimous agreement on the need for 'regeneration', what this actually means is less clear. This much was demonstrated by strong local opposition to the London Regeneration Consortium's and British Rail's proposals for a corporate-led approach to the redevelopment of the area in the early 1990s.

Contemporary King's Cross is in a constant state of flux, characterised by movement, defined by its railway termini, underground station and cross roads. This feature is often cited as being largely responsible for the problems ascribed to the area. However, the scale of the development opportunity the railwaylands offers determines that wholesale change is possible, leaving the area open to projections of utopian city environments which favour a 'clean sweep' approach to urbanism. While the developers' recent publications state their intention to deliver a 'mixed use' environment characterised by variation and diversity, on their terms it would seem that such an environment has to be forced. The emphasis in their recent literature portrays the existing environment as 'very fragmented and disconnected' (Argent St. George, 2002: 11).

It is significant that the only collection of essays on the subject of the history of King's Cross is entitled *Change at King's Cross from 1800 to the Present* (Hunter and Thorne, 1990). Notably, the area does not feature in recent accounts which attempt an all-encompassing history or 'biography' of London, and where it does feature, the emphasis is limited to the landmark architecture of the two stations.[4] Hunter and Thorne's collection of essays is dominated by stories of dramatic urban transformation – from the rapid speculative residential development of the area in the late eighteenth and early nineteenth centuries, to large-scale infrastructural change like that initiated by the railways. These are accounts of urban adjustment determined from above, or from outside and justified through reference to the good of the city as a whole – London's legibility on a national scale, in the case of the railways; or social and economic status, made legible through architectural means, in the case of the history of residential development in King's Cross. We might well ask how far a constantly shifting urban environment such as this can ever really be 'legibile'.

Previously known as Battlebridge, King's Cross took its name from a monument built to George IV, completed in 1836 and taken down by 1842.[5] The name survived the monument, which was the subject of immediate criticism, and which in its short history underwent a functional morphosis, ironic in hindsight, from national monument, to police station, to public house, before it was eventually demolished. That the name of the area derives from this monument, with its unlikely range of civic functions, is indicative of the complexity of the construction of the multiple identities (and thus legibilities) of the area. In a very practical way the history of the King's Cross demonstrates that architectural and urban legibility frequently and inevitably override initial design intentions and require flexibility of function, interpretation and use; the monument exemplifies the slippage between the built urban fabric and notions and perceptions of place and identity.

The monument introduces the idea that legibility is attached to the naming of an area, to identity; and that King's Cross, from one perspective (usually outside of the locality and local population) has been considered as a part of the city subject to many crises of identity. These perceived crises have led to numerous attempts at 'improvement' and to the area being positioned as somehow other to the rest of the city, a 'landscape of exclusion' in David Sibley's terminology (Sibley, 1992). For example, take the following quotation from The Mirror of 1833:

> Descending Pentonville Hill you will find yourself at Battlebridge among a people as characteristic and looking as local as if the spot had been made for them, and they for the spot. It is the grand centre for dustmen, scavengers, horse and dog stealers, knackermen, brickmen, and other low but necessary professions...the neighbourhood, however, is improving, and its poorer dwellers are getting gradually pushed further into the background – out of sight, but not out of reach of another faculty if you have a nose with its sense unimpaired (The Mirror, 1833, vol. 5: 425, 427).

This perception of the locality sees the 'problem' of the area in terms of its population, those 'low but necessary' professionals living in King's Cross, attached to the area as a result of their association with industrial activity. With hindsight, the sentiment expressed by the author – that the area is dirty and undesirable, and in need of a 'clean sweep' – takes on a new significance in light of the fact that the term 'gentrification' was first applied in urban sociology by Ruth Glass, working at the time in Flaxman Terrace, King's Cross (Mutale and Edwards, 2002: 2, n. 2). The description suggests both the long association of the area with activities and people perceived as abject, through an image of bodily repulsion to the area, and the continuous attempts at improvement that it has been subjected to, through the physical and social cleansing of the urban environment and population: regeneration efforts to counteract perceived degeneration.

Reading King's Cross

In discussing the image of King's Cross, we might remind ourselves of Lynch's assertion that the London constructed through the novels of Charles Dickens is as 'real' as the built urban fabric and thus contributes to the legibility of the experience of the city. This idea has recently been developed in the work of James Donald who contends that:

> The novel teaches us how to see the city, how to make sense of it. It defines the co-ordinates of our imaginative mapping of urban space (Donald, 1999: 2).

Smith's Dust Heap, end of Gray's Inn Road, King's Cross (courtesy of London Metropolitan Archives)

Combining all the elements of the nascent industrial capitalist city Dickens took as his themes – crime, pollution, congestion, noise and poverty; but equally texture, pleasure, fulfilment and opportunity – King's Cross formed the raw material for the setting of novels such as *Dombey and Sons* (1846), in which the author evoked a disorderly territory and converted this into his own linear narrative mapping of London. As Sophie Watson and Gary Bridge have recently written:

> Dickens…transposed the materiality, sensuality and texture of London into text…the themes of his novels resonate with salient urban issues of today – crime, law, streets, shops, transport, and popular pastimes or popular culture, and at the less tangible question of urban alienation (Bridge and Watson, 2002: 7).

This process of transposition takes the form of a reciprocal exchange whereby the literary image is itself projected back on to the urban fabric.

In his cultural history of dust, Joseph A. Amato interestingly asserts that dusts define 'much of the sight, feel and smell of urban life' (Amato, 2000: 9), indicating that physical urban dirt is culturally and historically specific, and determines the experience of the city. Equally, it seems, perceived or imagined dirt has an affect on the image of city districts. In popular perception the image of King's Cross owes much to Dickens' evocation of dirt and disorder, a narrative of urban decay through which he navigates the reader. The 'suburban Sahara' described by Dickens in *Our Mutual Friend* (1864) is a landscape where dirt and rubbish form the co-ordinates through which the city is mapped. Dickens drew particularly on the dust heaps which characterised the area.[6]

Smith's Dust Heap was the most monumental of these, sitting at the northern end of Grays' Inn Road where it accumulated in the early nineteenth century, opposite the Smallpox Hospital (Aston, 1998: 1–2). Comprised of dust, ash and cinder – used in brick-making – the mound has been argued to be partly to blame for the area's insalubrious character relative to the southern side of the New (now Euston) Road.

Dickens' emphasis on the 'dirty' aspects of the urban topography finds more recent parallels in contemporary literary representations of King's Cross. In Salman Rushdie's depiction of the area in The Satanic Verses (1997), for example, and even more recently in Phil Shoenfelt's Junkie Love (2001) in which King's Cross becomes the setting for a fictional narrative of lives dominated by drugs and crime. Shoenfelt describes the 'the red-light district in the backstreets behind King's Cross station, a place where the most fucked-up and hopeless street whores in London worked, and where only the punters in need of a serious sleeze fix went' (Shöenfelt, 2001: 96). Rushdie's description of St. Pancras and the gasholders portrays a similarly hopeless environment, where local landmarks representative of past industrial power and civic stability have accumulated the negative associations of an area deemed to be dirty, dangerous and disorderly; notorious for street prostitution, the drugs market and associated crime. Both authors construct a negative image of the area which echoes the extreme image projected in contemporary local and national media representation.[7] Furthermore, these negative, at times dystopian, projections are invoked in the discourse surrounding regeneration, where an imaginative paradox of 'the dystopian city as the seedbed of a potential urban utopia' comes into play (Baeten, 2002: 114). As Guy Baeten has argued, a 'hypochondriac geography' emerges whereby parts of the city are imagined through a 'peculiar epistemological framework of problems'. The proliferation of negative images such as these has given the area a particularly clear legibility, or at least recognizability, in recent decades, if not in Lynch's understanding of legibility. At times, contemporary re-branding attempts which have aimed to reverse such associations as these seem simultaneously to have re-confirmed them.

In the following part of the paper two architectural projects, both intended to contribute to the regeneration process, will be elaborated as case studies, interpreted as contrasting responses to the perceived 'dirt' and problems through which King's Cross has been categorized as an established city 'district' in Lynch's classification (Lynch, 1960: 67). Lynch describes various characteristics including 'maintenance' as a 'thematic continuity' which may contribute to the determination of the identity of a district. The physical attributes of definition which he describes are in turn represented and reconstructed through means other than the actual urban fabric, and these representations and reconstructions themselves affect the perception of the image of the district.

The British Library: Legibility, Control and Containment

...if architecture is in the business of producing 'order', it is involved in something far bigger than it can possibly handle, the process by which experience is filtered, transformed and fed back to us in reduced form, all in the name of 'culture' (Forty, 2000: 248).

The British Library designed by Colin St. John Wilson (1974 – 1998), showing Sir Isaac Newton (photograph by Ben Campkin)

For the writer Iain Sinclair, the British Library is a 'locked cellar of words' and a source of dark mystical power (Sinclair quoted in Barry, 2000: 190). These two images may be read as the opposite of the one intended – firstly, that the library is a public collection, maintained in the interests of the nation and therefore of each individual citizen; and secondly, that as a monument it 'touches the hem of the sacred' (St. John Wilson, 1998: 7), and is therefore a source of power but in the most morally pure manifestation possible. As a landmark building the Library presents itself to the outside world as a defensive object. The architect, Colin St. John Wilson, has stated his objective of providing 'protection from the hubbub' and 'turmoil' of the street outside (St. John Wilson, 1998: 36). It might be argued that the role of a national library is necessarily a protective one. Knowledge is jealously guarded and, in the context of the British Library, in King's Cross, has to be even more so because of the perceived threat embodied in the external environment and its population. Passing under the guillotine-like main gate into a 'piazza' which forms a buffer zone between the street and the library, it is difficult not to sense this anxiety. The Library comes to represent the pure and 'healthy' mind, where classification systems are clearly established and threats to these systems are rejected with ease. The spatial arrangement determines a series of inward turns, a gradual compartmentalization, which dislocates the library user from the context of the city, from any sense of where he is in London.

Rather than being read as a system of protective enclosure, the actual experience of using the library borders on a 'xenophobic' spatiality of the type that Michel Foucault reads from the programme of the monastery, with its explicit definition of who belongs, their position in a precisely constructed community and of what happens when and where (Foucault, 1997: 376). In this sense the building is an example of architectural introspection. Despite the supposed intention of playing a role in the regeneration of King's Cross, it shuts itself off from the city outside.

Paradoxically, it is by evoking a sense of the street outside that the architect argues that the building's users will attain a sense of security about their own place, their own bodies, within the daunting architectural (and, we may infer, epistemological) space within.

> ...*the sheer size of the concourse is broken down to human scale by threading throughout the space an intermediary set of elements...canopies, carved seats and balustrades and the clusters of suspended lights assert a human scale much as street furniture...Above all bodily assurance draws upon a sense of mass* (St. John Wilson, 1998: 50).

However, the traditional open and public space of the piazza is substituted here by an enclosed and highly controlled environment (divided into 'smoking' and 'non-smoking' areas), conspicuously patrolled by guards and cameras, acting as a security barrier. Clearly, there is a need to protect the contents of the library and for the regulation of the interior environment, owing to its function. As a self-contained environment the Library is highly legible and works efficiently. However, in design terms there are just two gestures which might be viewed as an attempt to relate the building to its context in King's Cross: the red brick and staggered roofline both of which provide visual links with the neighbouring Midland Hotel and St. Pancras. Otherwise, the architecture purposefully dislocates the user from the city through a series of boundaries and barriers at once physical, social and psychological.

The most obvious manifestation in the library of the 'public mind' is the King's Library, displayed from the first floor and acting as a visual core for the public areas. The special nature of this part of the collection is signified through the dark interior finish of the case which contains it, contrasting with the rest of the foyer which mainly uses exterior finishes. Lit from within the case, its contents are highly visible – seemingly accessible, but ultimately untouchable: a second royal monument in King's Cross with a legibility that is not as straightforward as it might first have appeared. Designed over such a protracted period the Library as a symbolic building reflects something of the same anxiety evoked in Eduardo Paolozzi's sculpture of Sir Isaac Newton positioned in the piazza on the axes of the two entrances on Euston Road – an uncomfortably positioned Newton marking out territory with his dividers, a monstrously enlarged version of William Blake's image of the scientist but with added nuts and blots which allude to a future robotic age and artificial intelligence. In a similar way to Paolozzi's Newton the Library has 'out grown' its function and location, housing as it does a physical archive in a period of increasing mobility of information through telecommunication, where legibility of 'place' takes on new meanings.

The Almeida at King's Cross: Images of 'Dirt'

The temporary Almeida at King's Cross, designed by Haworth Tomkins Architects, opened in 2001 and closed in 2002. This building represents an approach to dealing with the image ascribed to contemporary King's Cross which contrasts with the design of the British Library and leads us directly into a discussion of contemporary regeneration and city legibility. The example is interesting from the point of view that it inverted the approach deployed in the British Library, so that we find the architects consciously enhancing and developing a narrative of images in the building that referred directly to the area's image as a red-light zone.

Vast in size but hidden from view between the Caledonian and Pentonville Roads, the building to be converted had previously been a car and bus garage; and immediately before the Almeida moved in it had acted as a shelter for the area's homeless population and a place for sex workers to bring their clients. Less a single coherent building than a collection of spaces, altered and added to piecemeal since the 1940s, this was run-down, neglected building stock, polluted with oil and exhaust stains. The conversion of the garage space was funded by King's Cross Partnership among other official agencies of regeneration. The site was taken on by the Almeida to use while its home in Islington was being refurbished, the company joining a contemporary trend in staging productions outside of the theatre proper, provoking a more acute awareness of the relation between production and site. The Almeida capitalised on this idea that theatre might not be so self-contained, spilling out from the stage in a reciprocal exchange where the image of the location would also flow back into the theatre's productions.

On the 1st of March 2001 the new temporary theatre opened with a newly written version of Frank Wedekind's *Lulu Plays*, first written in the 1890s and brought to a wide audience through the film *Pandora's Box* (1928), directed by Georg Wilhelm Pabst. Having planned to put on a performance of *Lulu* at the Old Vic Theatre, it was decided to move into the temporary accommodation in King's Cross, earlier than anticipated, because of the additional resonance that the play would have in this location, drawing a parallel between the plight of the central character, Lulu, and the sex workers in the area. Lulu is a *femme fatale* whose sexuality is defined in relation to the cities of Berlin, Paris and London, where she finally ends up. The tension between the fictional situation portrayed in the play and the uncomfortable reality of its being staged in an area considered to be a red-light district was played up by those involved with the production, particularly in the set designs for the closing scenes, where Lulu ends up working as a prostitute in east London where she is murdered by Jack the Ripper. The audience are led to make direct connections between what they are seeing and the grit of the city outside, via their sense of location. The theatre lacked the usual comforts associated with an auditorium, particularly any sense of tightly-sealed enclosure.

The Almeida at King's Cross, entrance at night. (Courtesy of Haworth Tomkins Architects)

Rather than hindering the suitability of the space to theatre, the signs of its previous use as a garage – dust, oily walls, worn floors – were *sealed in* for effect. Like Brutalism, this was architectural form used to invoke morality, good straightforward and honest intentions, through 'raw…aesthetic characteristics' (Shonfield, 2000: 20). One review of the building in the national press used the label 'punk or guttersnipe architecture'.[8] The architects liked this label because it suggested the notion of 'belonging to an underworld' and the idea of an 'architecture which falls between the cracks' (Campkin, 2001). They point out the analogy of a brothel, rendered mainly through the use of lighting and signage and through the concealment of the theatre in a narrow back street, so that the audience had to be aware of the geography of the area to locate the building.[9]

The plastic wall which ran to the entrance in Omega Street played with notions of containment; at night, when lit, the onlooker was taunted with the silhouettes of the audience visible through the wall; the edges were blurred between theatre and street, urban image and urban 'reality'.

In contrast to the design of the British Library, and to other designs which have formed part of past master plans to regenerate King's Cross – which arguably envisage regeneration through a total 'cleansing' of the area and its unwanted communities – Haworth Tomkins's localized approach for the Almeida consciously played with ideas of streetlife, within the freedom offered by the context of a theatre project. In this way the building reinforced stereotypical images of the area as a 'seedy' environment, a location for illicit activities to take place within the city. *The Guardian* headline 'Nice and Sleezy: Almeida Brings a Touch of Class to Vice-Ridden King's Cross' emphasizes that the theatre was seen as an opportunity to benefit the area through a 'classy,' fashionable, cultural project. While exploiting the 'seedy' reputation of King's Cross, through a process of theatrical abstraction, the regeneration authorities who had funded the project were able to rest assured that it was only ever to be temporary.

An Area of Outstanding Unnatural Beauty: Legibility through Interaction

It must be granted that there is some value in mystification, labyrinth, or surprise in the environment. Many of us enjoy the House of Mirrors, and there is a certain charm in…crooked streets…This is so, however, only under two conditions. First, there must be no danger of losing basic form or orientation, of never coming out. The surprise must occur in an over-all framework, the confusions must be small regions in a visible whole. Furthermore, the labyrinth or mystery must in itself have some form that can be explored and in time be apprehended. Complete chaos without hint of connection is never pleasurable (Lynch, 1960: 6).

The things that make cities are invisible, and whatever is visible is seldom legible (Richard Wentworth).

Conceived by Richard Wentworth and Artangel, *An Area of Outstanding Unnatural Beauty* (2002) consisted of a site-specific installation in a vacant plumbing warehouse which became the point of departure for a series of walks, talks, games and other events, encouraging interaction with the history, identity and mapping of King's Cross. In this and earlier projects, Wentworth's interest is in how we experience, view, map and animate the city, and how these processes overlap and inform one another. The project itself is difficult to describe – impossible to describe in its totality – because of the diverse range of elements of which it was composed. The numerous events, conversations, walks and talks that took place – and continue to take place – defy the limits of a linear text. However, here I will try and outline a few of the components of which the project was made up in terms of what they suggest about legibility and the city.

The title of the project itself, *An Area of Outstanding Unnatural Beauty*, suggests the artist's interest in the identity of King's Cross and people's perceptions of that identity. Here, as with past Artangel projects – Rachel Whiteread's *House* (1993) in east London, for example – the site and the work are inextricably linked; and also like *House*, the focus of impending change and redevelopment. The title mimics the tag normally given to areas labelled as having a particular natural beauty and the inversion of this tag prompts us to consider how such judgements are determined and, indeed, what might be considered 'beautiful' in this most pronouncedly urban context, in an area generally represented, as we have seen, as undesirable and dirty. We might at first think that Wentworth has a preservationist or conservationist attitude to the area and is moralizing about the impending transformation but the point rather seems simply to ask us to reconsider a territory with which we already think we are familiar. To make something that at first appears to be clearly legible momentarily illegible. Rather than view an exhibition about King's Cross, Wentworth seemed to be asking visitors to explore and experience King's Cross itself.

The installation was based at a former General Plumbing Supplies store on York Way, formerly Maiden Lane, King's Cross. This ancient road was previously the boundary between the boroughs of Islington and St. Pancras. Close to the Regent's Canal, and facing west towards the Channel Tunnel Rail Link redevelopment site, the building is characteristic of mid-twentieth century light industrial architecture in King's Cross – characteristic, that is, in its ordinariness. Though the entire façade of this building had been painted, prior to Wentworth's occupation of it, with the American flag, this only served to camouflage it in King's Cross, where such visual incongruities are a matter of course. It is typical of the artist to have made a statement of such architectural understatement. The large sliding metal opening to the plumbing workshop provided a wide informal entrance to the installation space inside, contrasting with the usual ritualised transition which occurs on entering an art exhibition space, literally bringing the street inside, diffusing the boundary between the art and its location.

As opposed to the formal visual and spatial programme of an exhibition, the linear narrative which makes it legible according to the curator's will, the visitor to General Plumbing Supplies was confronted with a bizarrely incoherent arrangement of apparently incongruous objects and images. Within the large 'L'-shaped interior of the building this collection of objects and images included: a large A-Z map of London on which visitors could pin the location of their house or place of work; a set of table tennis tables on which parts of an enlarged A-Z map of King's Cross had been painted;

Interior of General Plumbling Supplies during **An Area of Outstanding Unnatural Beauty.**
(Courtesy of Art Angel and Richard Wentworth)

an up-turned shipping container fitted with a staircase leading up to a periscope which looked out over the rooftops of King's Cross; various maps of the area ranging from aviation maps of London and aerial photographs of the area to maps charting the local frog population. A number of films ran on various television screens found in the area by the artist. These ranged from a film taken by a natural history film photographer of the A-Z being made by hand as it was before more modern technological methods were deployed; to a film of directions and lines being painted onto the road; to a film of the vapour trail following an aeroplane crossing London. In addition, the Ealing Comedy *The Lady Killers* (1955), set in King's Cross, and *A Matter of Life and Death* (1946) directed by Powell and Pressburger ran alternately, their respective soundtracks reverberating through the space. Various full-length moveable mirrors were positioned throughout the building at floor level and from the roof trusses. Painted in white as directions are painted on the road, the title of the project ran diagonally through the space. In addition, other features remained in the space, to varying degrees rearranged or emphasized by Wentworth, from its time as a plumbing workshop, creating a surreal sense of an extraordinary environment.

Each of these elements might be interpreted as having had something to say about how we experience, move through and understand King's Cross in its present state of flux, but equally the visitor was prompted to consider the history and future of the area. Though certain objects and images might have refered specifically to Wentworth's own imaginative conception of King's Cross, tracing these individual references in the work does not seem important. Rather, it was with the questions the objects and their location provoked about King's Cross that the visitor was being encouraged to engage.

The question of the meaning of individual objects within the installation was downplayed while the collective set of objects and the space in which they were set prompted the visitor to consider the impossibly complex relationship between the city and its meanings except through the active participation of its individual inhabitants as subjective 'readers'.

Contrasting with the static maps of King's Cross posted on the wall of the plumbing workshop, enlarged maps painted on to table tennis tables over which visitors were encouraged to play ping pong[10] communicated ideas about the animation of space in the area through daily movement patterns. This basic metaphor for the circulation of people and vehicles through the area could be understood by the visitor without further explanation. The visitor who then went on to sit in front of the film *A Matter of Life and Death* may also have understood the ping pong theme as a reference to that film, where the game is used as a device for expressing the dialogue and conflict of interest between two of the main characters. The ping pong maps bring home the subjective and localized aspects of city legibility in the context of King's Cross. Legibility in this context is both visual and tactile and produced through interaction; in this sense the legibility of King's Cross is seen in terms of possession, through continuous dialogue: negotiation and renegotiation.

> The pleasure of the street for me is that it's out of control, it's a kind of free theatre
> (Wentworth, 2001: 413).

As a collection of disparate things and ideas, Wentworth's project challenged our understanding of the legibility of King's Cross by prompting us to think about how incoherent our image of the city is, animating apparently objective cartographic representations of the area through juxtaposition with fictional and intentionally disorientating images and objects. As we have seen from novels such as Phil Shoenfelt's *Junkie Love*, King's Cross has frequently been represented as a disorderly environment in the popular imagination. Caught between this and the future possibility of a commercially pre-determined – yet illogical? – legibility, Wentworth's project raises questions about how we conceive of legibility in the context of the city and highlights the role of individual city users as active participants in shaping urban experience. Rather than prescribing or imposing one particular view of the area, reinforcing or ignoring specific aspects of its history and identity, or romanticizing about its past, present or future, Wentworth's project initiated individual and collaborative exploration of King's Cross, facilitated through diverse points of departure. Furthermore, the work emphasises that design professionals in the built environment do not have sole power and responsibility in regulating the city but that legibility is primarily reliant on individual and subjective processes.

Conclusion

King's Cross in its past, present and future states poses some specific questions regarding the legibility of the city relevant on both a conceptual and a practical level to contemporary urban studies. The three examples elaborated in this paper indicate three distinct readings of King's Cross, responding to the perceived need to change the identity of the area in wholly different ways. The examples of the British Library and the temporary Almeida Theatre at King's Cross elaborate alternative approaches to the legibility of the area through design tactics which respectively reject or embrace its existing identity; the resulting designs are clearly driven by the scale and function of each building – on the one hand a national library, on the other a temporary theatre. Ultimately, however, each building is organized around an abstract urban imagery, which by turns excludes or embraces the image of the area.

The regeneration body, King's Cross Partnership, has recently erected brightly coloured hoardings over the frontages of Victorian buildings on the Caledonian Road and elsewhere in King's Cross. These display the slogans 'King's Cross: Take Another Look', and 'The Changing Face of King's Cross', next to glossy images of green spaces, historic buildings and other images which attempt to communicate a changing city identity. These hoardings block spaces previously inhabited by citizens considered less desirable than those represented in the marketing imagery – the drug users, the homeless and the sex workers with which the area has become associated. As an instance of the re-branding of an area this suggests a potential danger whereby social considerations are neglected in the pursuit a particular type of formal legibility. The developers' recent document *A Framework for Regeneration* (2002), outlining their proposals for the main King's Cross Central site, may be correct to define some of the problems of the area in terms of its visual and spatial incoherence. However, the legibility of the process of consultation is brought into question when the overall framework including routes of transport and movement, public spaces and distinct plots of land for redevelopment are presented as pre-determined (Parkes, 2002). The specific threat to King's Cross seems to be a developer-led interpretation of legibility which will result in a formal urban 'logic' dominated by corporate interests at the expense of all else, which naively relocates the sources of the area's perceived problems and results in an over-regulated and underused environment which is anything but the 'mixed-use' 'diverse' city Argent St. George has claimed it would to achieve.

References

Anon, (1993) *Camden and St. Pancras Chronicle*, 4th February.

Ackroyd, P. (2001) *London: The Biography*, London: Doubleday.

Amato, J. (2000) *Dust: A History of the Small and Invisible*, London: University of California Press.

Argent St. George. (2002) *A Framework for Regeneration*, London.

Aston, M. (1998) 'The Dust Heap at King's Cross', unpublished typescript, January 1998, pamphlet 46.351, Camden Local Studies and Archives Centre.

Baeten, G. (2002) 'Hypochondriac geographies of the city and the new urban dystopia: coming to terms with the 'other' city,' *CITY* vol 6, no. 1, pp.103–116.

Barry, P. (2000) '"Take your shoes off in King's Cross": envisioning London', in *Contemporary British Poetry and the City*, Manchester: Manchester University Press.

Bridge, G. and Watson, S. (eds.), (2002) *The Blackwell City Reader* Malden and Oxford: Blackwell Publishing.

Campkin, B. (2001) interview with Steve Tomkins and Roger Watts, Haworth Tomkins Architects, unpublished, 6 August 2001.

Catterall, B. (2000) 'Informational Cities: Beyond Dualism and Toward Reconstruction,' in Watson, S. and Bridge, G. (eds.), *A Companion to the City*, Oxford: Blackwell Publishers.

Donald, J. (1999), *Imagining the Modern City*, London: The Althone Press.

Forty, A. (2000) *Words and Buildings. A Vocabulary of Modern Architecture*, London: Thames and Hudson.

Foucault, M. 'Space, Knowledge and Power', interview with Paul Rabinow in Neil Leach (ed.). (1997) *Rethinking Architecture: A Reader in Cultural Theor.*, London and New York: Routledge, pp. 367-379.

The Guardian (2001) 'Nice and Sleazy: The Almeida Brings a Touch of Class to Vice-Ridden King's Cross', April 2001.

Hibbert, C. (1969) *London: The Biography of a City*. London: Penguin.

Hodgkinson, P. (1997) 'The Two minds of Architecture: The Quick and the Dead', *The Journal of Architecture*, vol 2, Winter 1997, pp. 337-353.

Hunter, M. and Thorne, R. (eds.). (1990) *Change at King's Cross from 1800 to the Present*. London: Historical Publications.

Leach, N. (ed.). (1997) *Rethinking Architecture: A Reader in Cultural Theory*. London and New York: Routledge.

Lynch, K. (1960) *The Image of the City*. Cambridge, MA and London: MIT Press.

Mutale, E. and Edwards, M. (2002) 'King's Cross Regeneration,' unpublished report produced for the King's Cross Partnership.

Parkes, M. (2002) 'Briefing Paper on *A Framework for Regeneration*', http://www.bartlett.ucl.ac.uk/planning/information/texts

Shöenfelt, P. (2001) *Junkie Love*, Prague: Twisted Spoon Press.

Shonfield, K. (2000) *Walls Have Feelings: Architecture, Film and the City*, London: Routledge.

Sibley, D. (1992) 'Outsiders in Society and Space,' in Anderson, K. and Gale, F. (eds.). *Inventing Places: Studies in Cultural Geography*. Melbourne: Longman Cheshire, pp. 107-122.

St. John Wilson, C. (1998) *The Design and Construction of the British Library*, London: The British Library.

Wentworth, R. '"The Accident of Where I Live" – Journeys on the Caledonian Road,' interview with Joe Kerr, in Borden, I., Kerr, J., Rendell, J. and Pivaro, A. (eds.). (2001) *The Unknown City: Contesting Architecture and Social Space*. Cambridge, MA and London: MIT Press, pp. 386-405.

Notes

1. I am grateful to Johan Andersson, Michael Edwards and Barbara Penner for comments on an earlier version of this paper, in part developed from a dissertation, 'Degeneration/Regeneration in King's Cross submitted for the award of M.Sc. Architectural History at the Bartlett School of Graduate Studies, UCL (2001).

2. As outlined in his influential book, *The Image of the City*.

3. Bob Catterall in 'Informational Cities: Beyond Dualism and Toward Reconstruction,' in Watson and Bridge, *A Companion to the City* p. 198, poses the question: 'Is it correct to perceive sites like the King's Cross Railwaylands...as the developers do, as derelict and degraded property which unquestionably needs "renewal"?'

4. For example, see Peter Ackroyd's *London: The Biography* or Christopher Hibbert's *London: The Biography of a City*.

5. The monument stood 60 feet high at the junction of the New Road, Maiden Lane and Gray's Inn Road. Gavin Stamp, 'From Battle Bridge to King's Cross: Urban Fabric and Change', in Hunter and Thorne *Change at King's Cross from 1800 to the Present* p. 11

6   The dust heaps remained until they were removed to clear the way for speculative housing development in the second quarter of the nineteenth century. Gavin Stamp, ''From Battlebridge to King's Cross'.

7   The headline in the *Camden and St. Pancras Chronicle*, 'King's Cross labelled the "scrapheap of London"' is typical
of
      regular references in the local press to the abject, and the vice, dirt and disorder ascribed to it. *Camden and St. Pancras Chronicle*, 4 February 1993.

8   *The Guardian*, 'Nice and Sleazy: The Almeida Brings a Touch of Class to Vice-Ridden King's Cross', April 2001.

9   The architects had originally applied for planning permission to place sign posts to the theatre on the street, but permission was refused. In hindsight they say that they are happy with this decision, preferring that the building remain partially hidden until one approaches and is attracted towards the entrance by its powerful axial presence, emphasized through the lighting of the building at night.

10   One of the events associated with the installation was an ongoing table tennis tournament with teams of local residents and businesses competing against one another.

Esther Salamon

Cargo

A Pan-European Artists' Residency and Commissioning Programme
Examining Changing Working Practices and Regeneration Issues[1]

Introduction

The Nineteenth Century saying that a north countryman's idea of the four quarters of the globe were 'Roosha, Proosha, Memel and Shields' was not without foundation. Every year, as soon as the ice began to disappear from its surface, a great procession of deep-laden sailing vessels would set out from the coal ports of the North East Coast, bound for the Baltic. [2]

Cargo is centred on a programme of artists' residencies and commissions in three European countries – England, Latvia and Sweden. All are located along the North Sea/Baltic Sea, with strong maritime and trading connections, and each has undergone substantial social, economic and environmental change.

The project's aims are to:
- explore the socio-cultural dynamics between the workplace and the communities that sustain them
- explore notions of collective and individual identity in relation to the social, political, economic, environmental and cultural changes that these areas have undergone over the past thirty years
- examine the commonality and differences of working practices and regeneration strategies at a time when the workplace is no longer intrinsically linked to the community of its surrounding geographical area and where employment opportunities are becoming increasingly global and diversified.

As a conceptual framework, the project is focused on the geographic and economic links around the North and Baltic Seas which, from the fourteenth century, were consolidated by the Hanseatic League.[3] During this period, trade routes, monopolies and partnerships in several regions of Europe developed and thrived, many of which are continuing today through, for example, the European Union.

In recent years, working practices have been affected by changes in the way merchandise is bought, sold and traded. For example, ports are increasingly investing in sophisticated ICT and warehousing systems and this is having a marked economic and social impact.

> The Port of Tyne is further enhancing its multimodal transport hub with the installation of a sophisticated warehouse system, which will provide improved supply chain control through better stock control and traceability. Over seven hectares of port-operated, Customs-approved warehousing, will be radio-linked to allow operatives to carry out their workload quickly and efficiently while keeping in constant contact with the administration office. The system will control replenishment of picking faces, picking onto pallets and full control dispatches. Customers will also have the ability to view stock and place orders via the Internet, creating substantial cost and time efficiencies.

Equally, an expanded and increasingly accessible internet and deregulated telephone industry is resulting in major changes to global communication and to communities. Just as the internet has overcome distance in telecommunications, container shipping has negated distance in manufacturing – in 2001 the Port of Tyne reported a 50% increase in container volumes.[4]

The effect of these developments on the workplace, the community and the individual has been particularly acute in the selected locations of *Cargo*. Historically, manual and semi-skilled labourers lived near their place of work – the port, the fish quay, the shipyard, the coal fired power generator or the coal mine. The industry was in the heart of the village or town, alongside the church, school, shop, tavern and housing. Generally speaking, residents of the town shared common identities and views of the world.

These identities are currently in flux; they are being reconfigured and are, in some cases, in crisis. It is an increasingly diversified world, where lives and relationships are rapidly changing. In particular:
- the working environment
- the modes of production
- the role of villages, towns and cities
- communication of ideas, knowledge and emotions

These changes have principally been driven by global economic and political forces, with the result that a substantial proportion of the population has been left feeling increasingly alienated and powerless. *Cargo* aims to provide an opportunity for people (i) to question and comment on the speed of change, (ii) to identify the impact of these changes on their lives, (iii) to imagine and articulate new realities and scenarios, (iv) to contribute to debates on regeneration, and (v) to inform policy-makers. It is anticipated that in this way people will be able to exert some control over their lives.

Involving artists in providing new insights on contemporary realities and new possibilities is central to the project.

> If we desire clarity of fact about social life, then perhaps we should turn to social science; if we wish clarity of meaning, then the systematic musings of social philosophers may be helpful. [...] The experience of a work of art is not so much a mirror of reality but an analogue for it. Artistic vision is not a substitute for social science and philosophy, but a complement to them. Whereas science and philosophy impose the order of knowledge, the

artist gives us wisdom that comes with the recognition of chaos.
(Sederberg, P.C., in 'The Artist and Political Vision', ed. Banber, B.R. and McGrath, M.S.G., 1982, p. 313)

The Project

The intention is that *Cargo* will provide both artists and the communities with the opportunity to identify, express and celebrate understandings of their individual and shared economic and social histories within the context of profound change – decline in traditional industries; increasing globalisation; the rapid development of sophisticated technologies and financial systems; geographical changes to national/international borders, political systems and cultural identities. *Cargo* aims to use creativity, art and culture to gain an understanding of these monumental changes. By exploring past traditions and future possibilities in imaginative and inventive ways, the project will provide insights into a metamorphosed Europe.

> *We must go forward…but we cannot kill the past in doing so, for the past is part of our identity and without our identity we are nothing.*[6]

Through an artists' residency and commissioning programme, *Cargo* is engaging communities along Northern European ports – in Sweden (Gothenburg), Latvia (Karosta) and North East England (Cambois and Tyne Dock)[5]. These communities are examining the major changes – social, political, environmental, economic and cultural - that each has experienced over several decades. At the core of *Cargo* is a commitment to designing and implementing the project in a customised and coherent way in each of the locations. The insights produced by the project will be expressed through three distinct and inter-related sets of activities:

I. Artists' Residency Programme

Cargo is centred on the active engagement of participants in a series of artists' residencies and workshops. Artists, along with employees, young people and older people, are producing new work which explores (i) what it means to work and/or live in their community, (ii) their visions of the future.

In **Cambois,**[6] filmmaker Trevor Hearing and poet Joan Johnston are collaborating on a film. Through creative writing and film workshops, they are encouraging people to recount old and new stories, which combine elements of documentary and fiction/fantasy, recalling the past and seeking out a new future. With help from the artists, participants are being encouraged to look at past, present and possible future worlds by exploring and debating:

- 'What is your earliest memory of Cambois?'[7]
- 'When I was young I believed…'
- 'When I was young I hoped…'
- 'Hello everyone, it's a long time since I left Cambois and what I miss most is…'

- 'What happens to you when the fog comes?'
- 'Who will live here after you?'
- 'What, if anything, should be built on the land after the chimneys come down?'[8]

In **Gothenburg**, on Sweden's west coast, multi-media artist Dan Fröberg is working with people in and around Lagerhuset, a former warehouse near the port. Fröberg's involvement in the project has been inspired by the sinking of the cargo-laden *Göteborg*[9] near its home port in the mid-eighteenth century. The ship was carrying spices, tea and Chinese blue porcelain following a two-year trading mission with China. In memory of the sinking, Fröberg has invited Chinese artist Sun Guojuan to collaborate on the project. Together, they will compose a 'sound atlas', that is, a guide to Gothenburg's and Kunming's (a Chinese port) life – its harbour, the city and the people. To explore additional concepts of 'cargo', short video pieces will also be produced.

Finally, Fröberg is co-ordinating and enabling artists, administrators, educators and young adults in an exploration of 'communication and transmission'. The team has posed several questions, including (i) how do ideas develop and (ii) how are they shared? Remnants of discarded texts and messages will be salvaged and will form new (short) stories. '*I will scan the wastebaskets in search of malfunctional communication, the thrown away sentences...*' (Fröberg)

Animator Sheila Graber is working with employees of the Port of Tyne Authority at **Tyne Dock, South Tyneside.** This key Authority, responsible for twenty-two miles along the River Tyne, has a wide range of responsibilities, principally to ensure procedures, policies and legislation are complied with.[10] Prior to *Cargo*, employees had not had the opportunity to become directly involved with a practising artist. Graber, who is from South Tyneside herself and whose father worked at the port, has been running film workshops – using a variety of materials including plasticine, chalk and pens – in the Authority's boardrooms and canteens. Over the weeks, coastguards, administration and canteen staff and dockers have all become involved with the project. Participants have been asked to:

- 'Build up a face that sums up the River Tyne'.
- 'Build up a face with very different results'.
- 'Show us their knowledge of the River Tyne'.

The group has been exploring the nature of work and the many changes and developments to working practices that have been experienced at the Port Authority. As part of this exploration, the metamorphoses of cargo – both people and goods – are being investigated, following their journeys across countries, continents and cultures.

Karosta, on the Latvian West Coast, is a suburban district north of the city of Liepaja. This significant port was built as a military harbour in the late nineteenth century by Tzar Alexander III and has, over the past 120 years, endured several political regimes that have espoused a variety of conflicting ideologies.

The Soviet period ended in 1994 when 19,000 soldiers marched out and left behind a population of 7,000 residents, mainly Russian speaking and with limited knowledge of Latvian culture or language.

New media artists involved with the K@2 Information and Cultural Centre intend to engage the local community in a substantial and intriguing lens-based project. Following several workshops, the project itself will take place over a 24-hour period. During that time participants will be asked to take images of their most interesting personal places in the town. These will be categorised by time and place, providing a subjective/qualitative survey of the area.

II. Commission Programme

Whereas the residencies are creating site-specific work through intensive involvement with the communities, a series of commissions, independent of the residencies, will provide additional perspectives on the issues raised.

One creative practitioner from the field of new media art/internet art will be commissioned to create new work in response to the overall theme of *Cargo*. This person will develop the project website and will facilitate a virtual chat-room and notice-board, providing a platform for the sharing of experiences, work, views and aspirations. To ensure that all of the partners are able to participate and discuss the work fully as it evolves, translators in four languages [11] will be engaged.

A contemporary composer will also be commissioned to produce a work for voice. It is envisaged the piece will be inspired by the varied musical and cultural traditions, as well as the expressed socio-economic realities and aspirations of the participating communities.

III. A Final Live Event

Cargo will culminate in a public event utilising satellite technology to link all four sites. This event will provide an opportunity to celebrate the shared learning and experiences that have resulted from the project. It will provide a platform to showcase the work and the views of the artists and the communities and will symbolise a new twentyfirst century way of working, trading and exchanging ideas and knowledge.

The work will be presented simultaneously at each location in each country through multi-media projections and will provide an opportunity to present and share the outcomes of the project with the largest possible audience.

The Evaluation

An entirely independent body will be engaged to evaluate the project. It will aim to identify the connections, contrasts and commonalties between the experiences of the different European Member States, and will assess the impact of regeneration strategies on local people in each of the locations.

The Centre for Cultural Policy and Management at Northumbria University, Newcastle upon Tyne, will be undertaking this evaluation. The purpose will be to assess the extent to which the aims and objectives have been met. That is, the evaluation will determine the extent to which:

• 	artists and communities, across international boundaries, have become involved in

the articulation of past and current economic and social conditions, and have developed visions for the future
- participants have been enabled to develop new skills
- artists have created new artworks
- policy makers have been informed about (the project's) contribution to regeneration
- artists have been informed about (the project's) contribution to creative practice and development

Observations
Although *Cargo* is not due to finish until Spring 2004, and no evaluation has yet been undertaken, there are still valuable lessons to be learned.

Artists
Participation in the project is having a marked effect on the participating artists.[12] Graber, for example, grew up near the River Tyne and produced several films which explore the life and the sounds along its banks. *Cargo* has provided her with the opportunity to critically engage with it once more, enabling her to '*re-engage with the river, to see it from different perspectives – through the eyes of the coast guard, the dockers, canteen staff and administration.*'

Personnel
Originally, *Cargo* was underpinned by three major themes: (i) 'modes of production' – energy, industry; (ii) 'cultural exchange' – trade, communities; and (iii) 'communication' – information, transmission. In order to develop work that was inspired by the globalisation and deregulation of the telephone industry, the organisers aimed to involve employees/employers of a major call centre in North East England. The intention was to involve the call centre, which employed over 3,000 people, as a major partner. This proved impossible due to the centre undergoing extensive changes in personnel. Although disappointing, it did not affect the aim or feel of the project.

Other changes to the original intention of the project were caused by the last minute decision of one of the original partners (Poland) not to take part. These were partly due to (i) a job change by the main contact in Gdansk, (ii) a change to the cultural partner organisation's priorities and policies, and (iii) political motivations. This withdrawal temporarily jeopardised the project's fundraising strategy and necessitated a revision to the timetable.

These experiences serve to highlight the dependence of such projects on the individuals involved and their susceptibility to sudden and unrelated change. The more complex a project – and the longer the lines of inter-connection – the more fragile it becomes.

Developing Trusting Relationships
Several of the artists working on *Cargo* believe it is important to have the time to 'grow into a project, organically'. Sufficient time and energy are needed to develop trusting

relationships with people from the community.

In a project such as *Cargo*, which involves diverse cultural organisations, cultures and artists, open and frequent communication between all of the partners is necessary to ensure there is mutual understanding and mutual respect.

Post-Project Development

There are many examples of art/community-based projects, similar to Cargo, that leave communities bereft once the funding ends and the originators leave. In order to develop a strategy that ensures participants do not feel undermined, become disillusioned, apathetic and/or angry, consideration needs to be given to sustaining the activity and/or developing additional cultural programmes, well in advance of the original project finishing.

Cargo aims to make a lasting impact on artists and the participating communities by:

- reaching across international boundaries and fostering inter-cultural understanding through the exchange and the cross-fertilisation of ideas amongst communities undergoing similar changes
- involving artists and communities in the articulation of current conditions and visions of the future
- creating new artworks
- enabling participants to learn a variety of new skills
- informing policy makers
- informing artists' creative practice

Notes

1   Cargo was initiated by Newcastle upon Tyne-based charity Helix Arts and is being managed in collaboration with key partners in North East England, Sweden and Latvia. Financial support has come from the key partners, Arts Council England, Helix Arts, Northumbria University and Northern Rock Foundation.

2   From the 'Dictionary of Tyne Sailing Ships – a record of merchant sailing ships owned, registered and built in the Port of Tyne from 1830–1930' by Richard E. Keys, published by the author in 1998. 'Roosha' and 'Proosha' refer, respectively, to Russia and Prussia. 'Memel' is a trading port on the Baltic coast of present-day Lithuania. 'Shields' refers to the ports of North and South Shields at the mouth of the River Tyne, in North East England.

3   The Hansa developed a strong network of trade with key cities and towns along the North and Baltic Seas. The monopoly, which essentially protected and controlled trade, principally traded in the products of the sea, farm, mine and forest – timber, fish, furs, wool and cloth.

4   As reported in the Summer 2001 supplement, 'Tyneside Vision', in Newcastle upon Tyne's local newspaper in North East England, 'The Journal'.

5   Partnerships with cultural organisations in each location have been developed by Helix Arts. Each organisation has agreed to manage the project in their area – Wansbeck District Council (Cambois), The Customs House Arts Centre – (Port of Tyne), K@2 Cultural and Information Centre (Karosta), Natverkstan Kultur i Vast (Gothenburg).

6   A geographically isolated former industrial town on the North Sea coast of less than 1,000 residents known for its coal-fired power station, port and, most recently, its on and offshore wind farms. The offshore

generators began operating in December 2000 and generate enough power for 3,000 homes. A renaissance that is centred on the continued development of environmentally sympathetic initiatives is anticipated: 'The North East, with its shipbuilding and repair, offshore and manufacturing history, plus its rivers, coast and ports, is seen as an ideal candidate to supply an emerging UK wind industry.' (The Journal), 18 September 2001.

7   This, and the six subsequent points, are taken from workshops led by writer Joan Johnston with people from Cambois.

8   The four 550 ft. chimneys from the coal-fired power station in the centre of Cambois dominate the skyline. A very large proportion of the population was once employed by the power station. It is now closed and is due for demolition in December 2003.

9   Gothenburg.

10   Since the demise of shipbuilding, regenerating both banks of the river has been a top priority in North East England and has resulted in the development of new housing and significant leisure and cultural facilities.

11   English, Latvian, Russian and Swedish

12   Project Evaluation Proposal prepared by the Centre for Cultural Policy and Management, Northumbria University, August 2003.

Bibliography

Barber, B. and McGrath, M. (eds.). (1982) The Artist and Political Vision. Transaction Inc.

Felshin, N. (1995) But is it Art? The Spirit of Art as Activism. Bay Press.

The Journal. Newcastle upon Tyne.

Keys, R. (1998) Dictionary of Tyne Sailing Ships.

Terkel, S. (1988). The Great Divide: Second Thoughts on the American Dream. Pantheon Books.

Anne Douglas

On the Edge: An Exploration of the Visual Arts
in Remote Rural Contexts of Northern Scotland

To Intervene
- to take a decisive or intrusive role in order to determine events
- to come or be among or between
- to occur between events or points in time
  New Collins Concise English Dictionary 1987

On the Edge[1] as Case Study

This case study is a programme of five visual art projects in northern Scotland with five regional partners that has come about through a research framework.[2] It demonstrates aspects of the dynamic of intervention largely focused by conversation among the participants in the process. Intervention, as an artistic tactic (De Certeau, 1998)[3], raises a number of significant questions that challenge a conventional understanding of how art is made and experienced, in particular the status of the artist as sole author, the artwork as the sole vehicle for exploring creativity and the audience as passive witnesses of the creative act.

The theatre director Richard Schechner suggests that artistic traditions are relative to specific cultural conditions and values.

> In the Western post-Renaissance traditions of art, the product is valued: works are hung, 'museumed', taped, filmed, 'videoed' – as if they could be rescued from time. But in other cultures, or at periods of Western culture, a better balance has been achieved between the 'being in' of art and its material products (Turner, 1988:8).

Schechner is discussing the work of the anthropologist Victor Turner, in particular Turner's reflections on the nature of performance in human societies. He notes that Turner valued the working, the doing, the experiential exhilaration of 'being in'. He looked for the 'minute particular' – the intrinsically unique flavour of this or that culture, subculture or individual.

In On the Edge 'being in' is evident in the development of projects through involvement of the individuals when the work might affect and also in the open ended, exploratory nature of the journey. Conversation allows the sharing to happen. 'Valuing the particular' is a key quality of the project content that draws on the specific way of life and concerns of individuals and organizations where the projects are located.

The Dynamic of Intervention in On the Edge

Our context, remote rural parts of northern Scotland, challenged us to think differently about what we were trying to do at a number of levels – in professional art practice, as dwellers in remote rural places (Miles, 2000), within the education and training of the artist and as a research community. We understood enough to know that we were seeking a sharper critical awareness of how the arts work within culture. We started to build new projects within remote rural places by drawing together the specifically local with wider spheres of influence, operating the different roles of the artist, the audience and the curator or producer of the project. This was a different way of working from earlier approaches that had reinforced the separation of these roles into professionalised hierarchies in which the artist determines an outcome that the audience receives or consumes.

Within the On the Edge research, the network of organizations[4] co-operate to develop and evaluate the programme of five visual art projects as a shared experience. The spine of the research is a series of workshops that takes place every spring and autumn. These workshops ensure that the strategic objectives of the research permeate the project activity. The research intervenes in professional practice through a series of carefully constructed questions. The critical perspective of the research tests and retests ideas and actions within the network of partners. This spine keeps the research activity relevant to itself. It also enables skills and tools to be exchanged and developed. A key role of this spine is to create 'an interval of freedom' (De Certeau, 1984) that questions received models of excellence.[5] The workshops are facilitated by the cultural policy researcher François Matarasso, who has acted as a critical advisor to the research and adds considerable experience of evaluation, in particular of social impact.

The Partner Challenge, the Project Idea and the Artist

The research team, experienced artist researchers,[6] invited each of the five partner organizations into conversation over time about how they would like to use the opportunity that the research presented. We intuitively started to build the projects within key challenges, not as a problem-solving exercise but as an opportunity to open up new ways in which the visual arts could become operative. These ways work across social relationships operating as a bridge *between* academe and non-academic worlds, *between* the project partners and the communities in which they are located, *between* the professional art sector and other cultural organizations, *between* global networks and local communities, *between* professional expertise and the knowledge of vernacular that comes from dwelling in a particular place, knowing through dwelling.

Each partner identified their key challenges within their relationship with the community or sector that the organization served.

> The Museum of Scottish Lighthouses (MSL), Fraserburgh, is a heritage site that is located on Kinnaird Head, Fraserburgh where Stevenson built a lighthouse within an 11th century tower. Although known Europe-wide for the technology of lighthouses, the museum has attracted little local attendance, particularly by young people.

The Scottish Sculpture Workshop (SSW), Lumsden, was established in the 70s as a modernist sculpture 'factory'. It is currently undergoing transformation into an international residency centre for artists and others interested in the visual environment. Its relationship with the small community of the village in which the workshop is located had been remote but the new focus of the organization could potentially be significantly enriched by being informed about traditional knowledge and local expertise.

The voluntary community arts organization, Deveron Arts, Huntly sought to develop a programme of challenging arts that would enable the town of Huntly to see itself with 'fresh eyes' with 'the town as a venue for the arts'. Deveron Arts wanted to investigate the potential of a 'Town Artist' who could mediate between the inhabitants and a programme of ambitious contemporary art projects.

Duff House, the outstation of the National Galleries for Scotland, in Banff had been restored to its 18th century splendour as a William Adams house to accommodate significant collections from other historic houses in Scotland. The Chamberlain, Charles Burnett, felt that the value and experience of the restoration process was of interest to his 'client body' but had become invisible by presenting Duff House as a conventional country house visitor attraction. He therefore wanted to use the research opportunity to explore the organisation's role as a centre of expertise in built heritage by investigating an appropriate 21st century response to the loss of a significant 16th century painted ceiling in the region.

Shetland College Textile and Design Department, Lerwick was concerned about the relationship between design and creativity and the traditional crafts of lace making and knitting. Where these traditional forms of making are significant to the economy of Shetland, they are not currently attracting young people because of the lack of design and responsiveness to contemporary lifestyles. How could the traditions be revalued in a way that would be sustainable by Shetland craftspeople in the future?

At this first level of interaction between the research team and partner organizations, the research space was read to different degrees as an opportunity to change or influence a set of beliefs and values about how a cultural organization was working within its own geographical location and social networks. The move was away from the kinds of homogenization that come with centralized systems of control towards valuing the potential for a different character both to the way the organisation was perceived as well as the nature of its role, by being responsive to specific local circumstances and individuals. Challenging these beliefs or values would, it was hoped, enable the organization to become more effective and thereby more sustainable as its relationship to (local) people or 'community' became more meaningful, more vital. At the very least, something would be learned by sharing the journey.

The Project Idea

Each challenge formed the basis of a project idea. I will use two examples to make this explicit.

David Bett, Director of the Museum of Scottish Lighthouses, rethought the museum's role. It had been a repository for the material culture of lighthouse keeping, supported by the experiences of keepers who act as guides within the museum space. A new perspective revealed the lighthouse as an expression of the relationship between technology and communication and enabled us to view the museum as part of a continuity and to create a vital link with the lives of young people in Fraserburgh, whose daily experiences are mediated by technologies of communication – text messaging for example. How might an artist work between the two sets of interests – that of the museum and that of the Fraserburgh youth – in a meaningful way?

Chris Fremantle, then Director of the Scottish Sculpture Workshop, focused on the significance of the organization being in that particular place of Lumsden and what that could mean in relation to the future both of SSW as well as that of the village. Lumsden is an agricultural community and yet the last tenant farmer to earn his living full time purely from farming, Pat Dunn, retired in May 2003. How might the process of dwelling in Lumsden become visible and meaningful within both Lumsden's and SSW's evolution and change? Chris identified marginal rural land as a shared issue between the people of the village and the nomadic artists visiting the organization within residencies. The project could be a catalyst for a second phase of the development of the village. In the nineteenth century the village was planned with a view to maintaining an agricultural workforce for the Clova estate. The twentyfirst century phase of development would be driven by culture. The role of the artist within the project would be to make visible processes of dwelling within the village as the life of individuals and organisations, such as Pat Dunn and SSW, changed over time and to identify key issues about public and private space.

Community as an Act of Forming Relationships

Our experience of defining community within the projects has shifted from a simplistic notion of a group of people who happen to live in the same geographical location to a more concise notion of the process by which we, as humans, group and regroup in complex interactions of belief and values that are dependent on where we are, physically and culturally. Within On the Edge community defines an active process of forming relationships through dialogue in and around making art, thereby arriving at values, rather than assuming that these pre-exist.

The On the Edge research intervenes in the everyday of the remote rural places in which the projects are raised by opening up a temporary space for deep consideration for what might or could be by the partners and the communities. The artists intervene in the emergent projects by interpreting the briefs through their own personalities and artistic vision and (in most cases) opening up the brief further – more ambitiously, in unexpected ways and in relationship with other participants including local farmers, youth leaders, housewives, young people, school teachers, owners of historic properties, historians, academics, knitters, crafts officers, retired people.[7] The resulting programme manifests a range of approaches and related qualities – masculine, feminine, fraternal, youthful, responsive, felt, anarchic, permeating, diffused, convivial and, at times, unnerving, disruptive, provocative and sometimes destructive. Judgements about these qualities are to an extent a matter of perspective.

Convivial and Diffused

The artist Gavin Renwick had worked with Chris Fremantle in an earlier project *Owergaeing* in 1998 that focused a sense of place with a group of younger artists, architects and designers by exploring Lumsden in depth through walking, drawing, photographing and interviewing local 'elders'. In many ways Gavin's approach in this earlier project had informed the On the Edge Inthrow project (2001 – present).

> *The intention was to explore how SSW could facilitate an environmental reorientation of the community linking archaeological and cultural landscapes through engaging with the oral tradition of the people that have occupied the landscape* [8] (Renwick 2003 :13).

As both artist and researcher, Gavin is engaged in the repositioning of knowledge and aesthetics directly in the context of human existence,[9] The project in Lumsden offered Gavin an opportunity to work in his own country, Scotland, with the key issue – the democratisation of the land.

The first phase of the project involved a number of actions that were effectively entry points into a discussion about land and inhabitation with different groups affected by changes in ownership. Pat Dunn's retirement as a farmer marked 'the re-incorporation of his farm into the estate, the final clearance of the landscape with everyone finally consolidated into the village' (ibid). Gavin conducted taped interviews with the village 'elders' such as Pat Dunn and recorded visits to a meeting of the Doric Society of traditional language, poetry and music. He identified Doric terms that were then threaded into the project as a way of developing its meaning – inthrow is the Doric for hearth, fireside and also *by means of, through the agency of*; the term *reekin' lums* or smoking chimneys is used to read the changing pattern of inhabitation within the landscape. The smoke signifies dwellings that originally were widely distributed across and within the estate and are now concentrated within the village. It also marks changes in forms of heating based on local resource consumption – wood, peat – to one (central heating) based on a commercial system consuming resources from Arabia, Latin America and Alaska in the form of oil. A key idea is the changing relationship between home and house, where home is an area of land or landscape instead of just a house and garden.

Gavin tracked events such as the *roup*[10] or farm sale of Pat Dunn's farm equipment. The young people of the village were engaged in photographing the inhabitants in exchange for help with constructing a *bogie cart*.[11] Inthrow leaflets were designed and distributed at the roup as a mechanism to communicate the intentions of the project and as a vehicle for obtaining a response. Gavin with Chris Fremantle initiated a music workshop with the DJ artist Norman Shaw, involving a group of young people from

Fig.1 Evidence of the artist Gavin Renwick's methods used in Inthrow, including Norman Shaw's music workshop, the Lumsden poster and Pat Dunn's peat cutting tools

the village who collected found 'sounds' from their daily environment (from their own swearing to the sound of cock crow) used as raw material for sound pieces and a music event held within a ruined *clachan* or farmstead above the village.

These small scale entry points were developed by Gavin interacting in a convivial way with the village by living there, by encountering people in the pub and in their homes, entering into the space of their everyday through an interest in their way of life – traditions of farming, of peat cutting and of language. The quiet building of confidence has grown into a more ambitious and long-term proposal of establishing an 'archive' of traditional knowledge for the village. This could be supported by an apprenticeship of a young villager to co-ordinate the 'archive' and work with SSW to evolve it. A related proposal is to form a feasibility group to assess the relevance of Land Reform legislation in Scotland to Lumsden.[12]

Conversation as a Tool

Dialogue established through conversations has been a key method within the On the Edge process. The critic and theorist Catharine Stimpson (Kramer,1994) defines conversation as a 'tool' of cultural democracy, 'a working technique for making relationships and agreements happen' (Kramer,1994:27). Stimpson asks us to imagine a circle of relationships of different kinds of conversations that range from 'consensus' at one point in the circle, in which individuals share the moral and intellectual basis for action, to 'conflict without rules' at its extreme opposite in which force dominates.[13] Conversation is a tool for making consensus and coalitions occur on the one hand and for setting the rules of contests or rule bound conflicts on the other. Stimpson is identifying conversation types within the context of multiculturalism. However, these qualities are also useful for understanding the kinds of relationships between participants in On the Edge. Quality of relationship and quality of intervention are closely allied. It is within dialogue through conversations that values that are often implicit at the beginning become clear and explicit.

The character of intervention in Inthrow is slow, immersive and convivial. Gavin Renwick describes this process as a 'process of raising consciousness'. The relationship between the research team with SSW as partner organization and Gavin Renwick has evolved through intense dialogue and the building of *consensus*, a series of exchanges operating within what is fundamentally a shared set of values. Differences of interpretation of the project have been shared and resolved within conversations that have enabled artist, partner organization and research team to adjust their perceptions of each other and nurture and enrich each stage as relationships grow within the project team and simultaneously with the village.[14]

As the project has progressed, it has gathered its own autonomy and independence from the research process through the short, medium and long term outcomes identified in the artist's interpretation of the brief.

Structured, Cathartic, Playful *and* Disruptive and Unnerving

A different set of qualities characterize the Langerin'[15] project on Shetland. Susan Benn, the artist involved, is the Director of Performing Arts Laboratories (PAL) that explores creative collaborations between, across and beyond disciplines. Susan was invited to design and direct a new collaborative 'Langerin' Lab' programme to bring traditional and contemporary hand and machine knitters of the Shetland Islands together with a group of artists, designers and academics, from a range of disciplines, to stimulate new work and new ways of working. The aim of the programme was to revalue the traditional forms of making within contemporary ways of living. Susan articulates her artistic approach as follows

> *As the director of PAL I create, with lots of other people, an environment in which new thinking and ways of working happen through collective chemistry. It is what I call the 'pressure cooker' factor.*

Certainly in the beginning there is a lot of discomfort and dislocation that make people ask
questions about their practice, about their place in the group, their core values as a person.
(On the Edge workshop 5, Lumsden, 9.10.03)

The eight day Lab was the result of several months of careful preparation working in partnership with the research team and partner organization Shetland College. It took place in May 2003, incubating a range of ideas within a creative experience. Within the space, a number of ideas were identified to be further developed, produced, exhibited, published and marketed by March 2004. The Langerin' Lab is currently being developed further in collaboration with Shetland College and with the practical encouragement of the Shetland Development Department and other local agencies, to provide an infrastructure which supports the ongoing work of the project.

The nature of the intervention in this project is unlike that of *Inthrow* in that it is highly structured and negotiated at every phase of its development. It encompasses different paces of working from fast moving catharsis to slow, thorough preparation and critical reflection. Like *Inthrow*, it is convivial, playful but through working together in groups rather than individual encounters.

The Lab methodology structures and formalizes a shared space of taking risks through individuals' creative production. By entering and participating in the space of the Lab, an individual participant has the opportunity to grow in the process though there is no guarantee that this will happen. There is acknowledgement of danger and discomfort. The cathartic and generative qualities of 'labness' resonate with Turner's discussions on the nature of performance in ritual, *open, unfinished, decentred, destablising and liminal (betwixt and between)*(Turner, 1988). Its impact is reflected in the individual feedback from the lab from two of the participants

> *I found I was looking at designing in new ways and producing work from a different*
> *perspective....This type of event is invaluable to designers in remote areas especially, as one*
> *tends to become disconnected from new thinking.*

> *One does tend to get possessive about one's ideas but the Lab showed me that mutual respect*
> *and open discussion is very beneficial. It struck me that group working with the right*
> *atmosphere actually increases the creativity of individuals.*

The quality of relationship in the Langerin' project has ranged from *consensus* based on shared values and empathy between the research team and artist to a *coalition* between research team, artist and partner organization. The evaluation process has provided a space for revealing disagreements that at times have been painful to resolve. There are sharp differences of expectations between the partner organization, on the one hand, and the research team and artist, on the other, expectations that have become clearer as the process has evolved. After a great deal of discussion we have arrived at the decision to acknowledge that different interests are operating within the shared space but that these differences are significant to understanding the dimensions of the issue at hand.[16] It is therefore important to continue to work together on the shared issue of

Fig. 2 The Langerin' Lab participants involved in experimental work and the evaluation blanket monitoring day-to-day experience of the Lab.

revaluing traditional forms of making. Stimpson defines this process of continuing through an acknowledgement of difference as a *coalition*.

The experience of the Langerin' project would indicate that the process of developing the projects through exploration is by no means *consensual*. Valuable learning takes place at points of experiencing real tension between different individuals and their perceptions.[17] The journey, like good research, has exposed deeper levels of questioning, not least the 'food chain' and infrastructure of the industry that needs to be understood in a complex way. Research provides opportunities for this understanding to be developed as part of practice.

Paradoxical and Opportunistic

Paradoxical aspects of intervention are clearly evident within the *Town Artist* project with Deveron Arts. The artist in this project, Lynn Millar, tested the notion of 'town artist' as a relatively long-term development i.e. beyond the norm of a three-month residency. Deveron Arts were seeking to find a different way of being an artist in relation to the community of a town who was neither a community artist nor a conventional artist in residence. The assumption underpinning this search for a different model was the uncomfortable set of choices posed by existing models. On the one hand, high involvement in the community was perceived as a loss of quality in artistic terms. On the other hand, quality in artistic practice was perceived as a lower level of involvement and relevance to the community of the town. Lynn Millar's role was to support 'the implementation of dedicated short-term artist in residence programmes of various artistic disciplines' developed by Deveron Arts. Lynn, as a local artist, is firmly located within the community of Huntly and therefore effectively part of the way of life of the town. Her presence would, it was hoped, secure the acceptability of other work by incoming artists.

The aim of the 'ambitious programme of projects' was to enable Huntly 'to see *itself* with fresh eyes' through the intervention of *professional* art practices acting as an injection of a different kind of energy. Lynn's appointment within the research framework presented an opportunity whereby all the participants – research, partner and artist might learn from the process.

As the artist's role became increasingly pragmatic, in terms of supporting and realizing the initiatives taken by the partner organization, it became evident that we were some way away from identifying 'a third way'. The artist became frustrated by the lack of clarity about what the role involved. Deveron Arts became frustrated by the apparent lack of real development in the role that they had defined as 'ideas maker and shaper'. The *Town Artist* project drew to a close after twelve months.

Despite the best intentions and some exciting work, these interesting concepts in and around the transformative role of the arts have tended to remain 'strap lines' or 'labels' used to attract funding. These have been very effective in generating projects. An area of real success within this project has been the development of mechanisms to stimulate debate on subjects such as 'rural commerce' and 'notions of home and identity' identified by individuals undertaking residencies. These events have been co-ordinated by the town artist. This level of engagement of the local community with formal debate initiated in relation to artistic practice points to an area of potential development for Deveron Arts and the community of Huntly.

The quality of conversation within this project between the partner organisation and the research team has been marked by *coerced conformity*, where the respective roles of partner organization, research and artists were enforced more by the 'legal', social and cultural definitions imposed on those roles than by trust, exploration and learning. Where for the most part the other four projects in the programme have developed conversation to 'help consensus and coalition to occur', within this project conversation helped to set up rules of engagement.[18]

Youthful and Anarchic

Within *Edge* FM project (partner organization Museum of Scottish Lighthouses) the artist, Paul Carter, bridged two systems of belief – that of the museum and that of a group of young people from Fraserburgh by building a radio station. In the artist's own words.

> Edge FM was run by a group of local young people who collected and transmitted the voices of people from the area talking about issues of identity. Using the radio broadcast to be heard and a museum exhibit to position themselves within the history of the town, the Edge FM project was the reclamation of the museum and of local history by the group (Carter, 2003).

The qualities of intervention in the *Edge* FM project are dynamic and improvised. The opportunity for young people to 'intervene' in the space of the museum was shaped by the desire of its director to encourage their presence and the skills of the artist in making something different happen through the vehicle of the radio broadcast and its development. The content – an exploration of identity, and its vehicle of dissemination, a radio station, interested the group of young skateboarders and BMX bikers enough to come together and to sustain their attendance over a series of weekend workshops. Paul's skill in creating a trust between himself and the participants enabled a unique kind of space in which the adult world listened instead of instructing, in which adults were challenged by and learned from what the young people chose to offer them and with which the adult world of the museum felt some discomfort. The young people relished the opportunity to invade the museum's space with their skills, the way in which they expressed themselves, their values and aspirations for the town's future. This sense of 'invasion' was carried through symbolically into the airwaves through the broadcast.

> In the city
> the bladers hate the skaters
> the skaters hate the bmxers
> but in a place like this
> abdy gets on
> abdy stick t'gither
> naebdy sees naebdy stuck
> (Fraserburgh 2 August 2003)

The preparedness to accept people for who they are is expressed by one of the participants in Edge FM, broadcast as part of the soundscape.

The relationships between research team, partner organisation and artist in *Edge FM* has been largely one of *consensus*, of agreeing on a course of action through fundamentally shared values. The Director of the Museum, David Bett, sought the support of community group leaders in Fraserburgh as a means of firmly locating the project within the experience of its young inhabitants. The artist's response was surprising but focused the project's aim more sharply than the team and partner could have envisaged. Paul stressed the importance of using 'low' technologies of radio (rather than the original idea of using contemporary digital media) because low technologies are more manageable and therefore empowering for the lay user, more could be expressed and more quality time spent on developing the broadcast. The energy of the young skaters and bikers proved quite challenging in the museum space, again stimulating new ideas about how the museum collection might be mediated in new ways to develop new audiences. Could skateboarding be choreographed into the task of guiding the public through the space? The broadcast produced rich insights into how concerned the young people were to marry local and global interests often expressed within their sporting interests. How might the museum lend itself to addressing these concerns in a lively way?

Dramatic and Complex, Spontaneous and Witty

In the Celestial ceiling project (partner organisation Duff House) the owners of a private space, Cullen House South Tower, raised the issue of the loss by fire of important Scottish heritage, the sixteenth century painted ceiling. Their initiative in bringing this issue to the *public* space of the museum led to a complex interpretation of the research opportunity – to raise two commissions with two different artists who would respond in distinctive ways to the loss. Robert Orchardson, a young Scottish visual artist, is in the process of 'replacing' the original ceiling with a new twentyfirst century painting. Through intervening in the original ceiling space he is appropriating the space in a new way and for his time. John McGeogh, a second artist, is developing a projected ceiling using new digital technology as a way of challenging the conventions of heritage interpretation by offering an artwork as a *new experience* of lost heritage, only possible through current technology. This artwork will tour to a number of historic properties.

The literal nature of the two commissions as interventions within architectural spaces belies another more, symbolic level of intervention where loss is transformed into creative opportunity. The values of the patron, of wit and spontaneity, open up the space in which new artistic content can play. The two artists have offered responses to these values that are witty and dramatic, improvising on the original content – a new celestial ceiling referencing yellow bath bubbles and astronauts on the one hand, and a Troy enlivened by animated flames and the individual portraits of the *putti*,[19] normally not visible to the 'naked eye', on the other.

Fig. 3 Spaces inside the museum created by *Edge FM*. Outside the building scaffolding was used to erect a radio mast for the one day licensed broadcast.

The relationship between 'actors' in this project has been demanding, businesslike, convivial and playful. It has been elegant and improvised. The research team has been highly active in the process of identifying artists, artistic approaches and content by co-ordinating discussions across interest groups. By each participant being open to the question 'Who should the artist be?', we have engaged in a process of learning from different 'experts' who have contributed to defining an approach. The rich material that has resulted from this process is available to the artists working on their respective outcomes within the conceptual framework of 'patronage'.

Conclusion

Focusing the On the Edge programme of projects by different qualities of conversation, *consensus, coalition* or *coercion*, has helped to recognize the needs of each project and the multiple strategies that have been required within the development, implementation and evaluation phases. These qualities have only become clear through the process of engagement, of 'being in' the process. What has actually happened is a result of a whole series of contingent factors in which each participant is part of a conversation. In this sense, culture is a 'co-operative adventure' (Harrison, 1985).

A clearly significant consequence of approaching the development of the visual arts in this way is the balance between what is taught and what is learned. Within the Langerin' project the learning is through sharing skills and experiences in which each participant is simultaneously teacher and learner. In contrast, within *The Town Artist* project with Deveron Arts project, the teaching follows a single trajectory. Both offer quite different types of exchanges.

What is the Role of Research Expertise in this Process?

The dynamic of intervention operative in the On the Edge projects is research led and simultaneously practice led. The practice is framed by questions to which nobody has the answers at the outset. Each participant in the process is at once the expert and also the non-expert. Each contribution is significant to a deeper understanding of the changing phenomena that we are trying to understand.

The research is instrumental in making the practice happen. It constitutes a powerful tool of creativity in culture. It is disinterested in the sense that Terry Eagleton suggests i.e. neither self-interested or self-orientated but trying to feel (a) way imaginatively into the experience of others (Eagleton, 2003). We do not apply specific genres of practice but embrace a complexity of approaches from ceiling painting (*Celestial Ceiling*) to projects that have no single artistic output (*Inthrow*) or (*Edge FM*), working across known genres of art. We also do not apply specific methodologies of research but position ourselves in a 'generalist' 'non-specialist' way in the same sense that artists are generalists using their skills of observation, empathy and communication to understand and represent experience in ways that can be understood by non artists.

The research and related practice is **self-critical** in the sense used by Jane Kramer, the American critic of public art i.e. the *local* figuring out of what works and what does not work (own emphasis) (Kramer, 1994). The development of evaluation processes

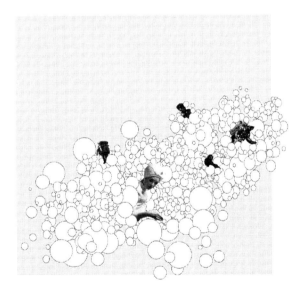

Fig. 4 A tiny detail from the tempera painted ceiling destroyed by a fire in 1986 and the proposal for a new painting on the ceiling by the artist Robert Orchardson. A second commission, a digital ceiling projection by the artist John McGeogh reinterprets the original ceiling and is planned to tour other heritage sites.

and tools that can be used as part of daily practice (and not just professional research) has been a key research outcome.

What Values are Created and Expressed by these Projects?

Within On the Edge it has been crucial to address the process of developing values from multiple perspectives – that of the partner organisation, that of the artists carrying out the work and that of the participants within the project 'sites' as well as the researchers who are also artists. Values are not a single truth. They are the subject of discussion, part of the act of forming or creating a sense of self in relation to others, intrinsic and central to the creative process.

Multiple perspectives can be contradictory and tense as well as shared. They engage thoughts and feelings that to one individual may be the subject of passion and to another, indifference. The complexity of possibilities is what is important as well as the space to reveal and explore this complexity and to learn from it. This learning stance is a different perspective from that of professional performance evidenced in the following ways.

The principal artists in each project have been invited in to contribute their experience and thinking by interpreting the project briefs and in discussing and sharing realisation with the partners, research team and participants. They are not asked to 'produce' but to 'participate in the production'. The artistic 'output' is positioned differently in relation to the process of development. In both Inthrow and Edge FM, for example, output is the least evident part of the process. The soundscape of Edge FM is a stage in a process of adjusting sensibilities and constructing new relationships between the young people and the museum. In contrast, in gallery or permanent public art practices, output is normally the most evident part. The means of disseminating the work is also different. Within sectors of professional visual arts practice dissemination conventionally takes the form of a glossy catalogue or academic text. On the Edge needs in this case to communicate to a different kind of 'lay' audience, including the range of participants in the projects, challenging us to evolve a different approach inspired by 'popular' or 'lay' culture – the information booklet or the comic.

Another manifestation of difference is the quality and intensity of relationships that are formed between people in remote rural areas in which mutual trust and interdependence is a question of survival. This is closely linked to sensitivity in relation to taking risks, the fear that failure is letting down the people that you know and depend upon. Project development is about judging risk in relation to personal relationships as opposed to an anonymous public.

This focus on relationship requires a different sensibility in relation to pace of development with different results. Where professional visual art practices in the gallery or in public art for example are regulated by the three week exhibition slot and new work or 'one off' project i.e. a 'professionalised' structure, projects in remote rural areas evolve slowly and painstakingly with people. (Each of the projects in On the Edge has taken a minimum of two and half years to build.) This process of nurturing relationship and ownership often leads to the seeding of co-developments such as those of Inthrow that could never have been fully envisaged at the outset but that map and rehearse the sustainable development of the activity.

Not every aspect of the programme is slow. There is also a need for catharsis, the injection of new energy that is short and sharp, evident for example in the *Langerin' Lab*. This catharsis needs to be supported by a framework or network of individuals who take on the responsibility of seeing the work through where in other contexts this responsibility might well be carried out by a single monolithic institution – the gallery, urban museum, public art organisation.

Finally, the nature of professional performance invests creativity solely within the role of artist. The On the Edge projects draw on the creativity of each participant to make the project work. The principal artist in each project facilitates and intensifies this process releasing new ways of being within the everyday.

Bibliography

Carter, P., (2003) *Bend Sinister.* Edinburgh: Fruitmarket Gallery.

De Certeau, M. (1984) *The Practice of Everyday Life* Trans. Steven Rendall. Berkeley: University of California Press.

De Certeau, M. Giard, L, Mayol, P. (1998) *The Practice of Everyday Life: vol. 2: Living and Cooking,* Trans T. J. Tomasik, Minneapolis: University of Minnesota Press.

Douglas, A. and Delday, H. (2003) *Adjusting Sensibilities: Researching Artistic Value 'On the Edge'* in publication for the European Academy of Design and The Design Journal.

Eagleton, T. (2003) *After Theory,* Basic Books.

Harrison, H. and N. (1985) *The Lagoon Cycle.* Herbert F. Johnson Museum of Art. Ithaca: Cornell University Press.

Kramer, J. (1994) *Whose Art is It?.* Durham and London: Duke University Press.

Miles, M. (2000) *The Uses of Decoration: Essays in the Architectural Everyday.* Chichester: John Wiley & Sons.

Renwick, G. (2003) *Inthrow: Artist's response to the On the Edge Brief,* unpublished research document. Gray's School of Art, Aberdeen

Turner, V. (1988) *The Anthropology of Performance,* Preface by Richard Schechner. London: Johns Hopkins University Press

Notes

1   The 'edge' is simultaneously a quality of remoteness as well as a metaphor for a creative challenge on a threshold between known mores of artistic practice and new forms of practice, a liminal space in which to suspend belief, to question and raise new critical frameworks.

2   The On the Edge research is supported by the Arts and Humanities Research Board (AHRB) 2001–4 www.ontheedgeresearch.org.

3   De Certeau's thinking is central to the On the Edge research project through the doctoral research of Heather Delday currently undertaking a studentship attached to the project. De Certeau distinguishes 'tactics' from 'strategies'. Tactics operate informally within the everyday as a fundamental creative tool of survival in contrast to strategies – the actions of the 'proper' or the given structures of power.

4   Including the Scottish Sculpture Workshop at Lumsden, The Museum of Scottish Lighthouses, Fraserburgh, Deveron Arts in Huntly, Duff House, the outstation to the National Galleries of Scotland, Banff in Aberdeenshire and Shetland College of Textiles and Design in Lerwick.

5   In workshops 3 and 5 a set of criteria were identified by the partners as relevant to their particular working situation. The results were different from received or externally imposed criteria by funders or major institutional perspectives such as the gallery, largely because they placed high value on the quality of process, the quality experience and the contribution of audience as a participant in the process.

6   Practice-led research is a space to be creative and reflective. The researcher both makes situations and makes sense of the experiences in rigorous ways by evolving practice and critical language together.

7   The artists that have the responsibility to carry out specific projects come on board in different ways. Some of the projects such as *Inthrow* (SSW) were formed with a particular artist in mind. In others such as Edge FM the principal artist was identified well into the process of development.

8   'The word culture originates in our relationship with earth, for its is with the agriculture that the landscape of the Scottish north-east was formed and delineated' (Renwick 2003 :13).

9   For a number of years he has worked in northern Canada among the Dogrib peoples as part of an interdisciplinary team that articulates the Dogrib notion of 'home' to the Canadian government with a view to sustaining the Dogrib way of life within the colonialism of western European Canada

10   *Roup* in the Concise Scots Dictionary means 'plunder, deprive of everything'.

11   A three wheeled cart made by teenagers out of improvised materials.

12   An ironic move given that the village was originally constructed by the adjacent Clova Estate to maintain a workforce in the area.

13   Other stages include coerced conformity, conformity, coalitions, contests, rule bound conflicts and conflicts without rules as different ways of reaching agreement or begging to differ.

14   For example, the music workshop with Norman Shaw came about as a result of rethinking the importance of young people and their experiences alongside that of the 'elders' of the village.

15   Langerin' is a Shetland term describing the getting together of women knitters in each others' homes to knit and share news and stories.

16   For example, Shetland College defines the lack of design in the knitting as a key problem though this has been implicit rather than explicit in the process of developing the Langerin' Lab. A narrow reading of the Lab as a mechanism for delivering this design element has led to real disappointment in the eyes of the partner organization in its outcomes, though this had never been an explicit objective of the project. Reading the Lab as a mechanism for encouraging a spirit of creativity and self-reliance within traditional knitters has produced a far richer set of results and processes that are less formal or nameable but that have seeded new ideas and collaborations that would never have come about without the catharsis of shared creativity.

17   Explored further in Douglas, and Delday: 2003.

18   Unlike the other projects, Deveron Arts interpreted the role of the research team as objective within the development process rather than participatory through a practice-led approach. For example, the artist was appointed without consultation with the research team.

19   cherubs

Andy Hewitt and Mel Jordan

I Fail to Agree

Introduction

Our recent projects have examined the function of art within economic and cultural systems in the UK; we have been concerned with the role of the artist and art within contemporary culture. In this text we have chosen to describe three of our projects. Within these works we attempt to examine the contradictions and the conflicts of interest between public and private agendas within regeneration objectives. Within the projects we also endeavour to discuss the functions given to art via government cultural policy and by the patronage of capital interests.

The projects took place over three years. As a result of working through the projects, we developed a further understanding of the issues; a revised consistency is not our intention here, so contradictions and discrepancies are present. When writing about your own work you can only really talk about the work in terms of context and outcomes, to make any qualitative judgements is very difficult. Therefore we have tried to concentrate on discussing our intentions and articulating our experiences.

We believe in the possibility of art having a role in the development and support of democratic systems. We are concerned that art continues to be appropriated and used for investment by capital and increasingly as a tool within government social policies. The dilemmas for the artist working between the powerful agendas of capital and government funding policy make it all the more urgent to maintain art as a space for thinking and for contesting authority and the prevailing culture.

Art practitioners, who for ideological reasons choose to work outside of the gallery market and seek to make art that is critical of capital and commodity, find that the public funding of art is equally problematic, having its own set of patrons and agendas. The public realm is becoming less public as capital interests have taken over more of what we once understood to be public. We see the 'subordination of society to capital'(Negri and Hardt, 1997) with capital orientated culture representing itself as alternative 'public' culture. Parallel to this a functionalist agenda within the public funding of art practice channels it towards the support of economic goals within culture-led regeneration and a 'third way' partnership with commercial concerns.

An art practice that develops an antagonistic relationship with these forces is one that risks being marginalized and unsustainable. Artists are faced with developing strategies to work around these agendas, avoiding becoming compliant whilst critically engaging with the place of art within a social and economic context. However difficult this is to maintains it is preferable to relinquishing the autonomy that is inherent to art.

The Projects

It is this 'culture of capital' that we attempt to investigate within our projects. Our practice is about questioning: confronting accepted systems, methods and approaches. We want to reveal that art and cultural systems are not benign but are deeply affected by political and ideological agendas. We believe in the arts as having some agency to support democratic systems but in order for this to be effective there is a need to fight for the control of its production and mediation.

The aim of recent projects has been to understand the role of art within the cultural industries, to see the function it has been given and the claims made about it. Our current preoccupations are with gentrification, the functionalisation of art within the branding of cities, and the conflicts of interest, between public and private, which take place within the cultural regeneration.

Our works often take the form of periods of research that allow us to operate within a particular context that interests us in order to develop a body of work. This method of working allows us to gain an understanding of issues that affect the context. The final output or outcome of our efforts, usually a visual work, will in some way represent our research and engagement. Our work often involves negotiation and discussion with a host organisation as we establish the basis of our collaboration and our methodology.

Ironically for us, a discursive art practice can become co-opted; it is attractive to commissioners, a consultative approach being close to those management techniques and quality assessment systems already in operation within government and business.

Artists are increasingly seen as a 'creative thinking' resource. This is reflected in the increase in artist commissions by a cross section of public agencies. It is commonly assumed that artists are there to assist in delivering your policy objectives and are just happy to get the work. The following projects reveal some of the ways in which art and artists are given a function within social and economic contexts.

'WINNER'

The project WINNER came from a period of research into the UK competition for the Capital of Culture 2008. The work examined the use of culture to brand a city as part of culture-led regeneration. The European Capital of Culture is a European Union agreement under which each year a member country takes its turn to select a host city to become Capital of Culture. After a long competition process Liverpool was, this year, selected to represent the UK as European Capital of Culture for the year 2008. During the run-up to the final selection we worked on a project entitled WINNER. We sought to understand why this competition was in operation, how each of the competing cities would interpret the word 'culture' and how the arts were going to function within any subsequent cultural strategy.

The competition was already promising to become a cultural phenomenon as an unprecedented twelve cities entered the UK competition. In August 2002, over a two-week period we visited each one. Birmingham > Cardiff > Bristol > Liverpool > Belfast > Oxford > Brighton > Canterbury > Norwich > Bradford > Newcastle > Inverness. Following on the heels of the official judges that included media and sports

WINNER The council chambers from the six cities short-listed for the Capital of Culture competition, 2002

celebrities, like Jeremy Irons and Tessa Sanderson, it was our aim to experience for ourselves the culture of each city. We met with people from the visual arts communities and representatives from city councils in order to find out what was being planned. Along the way we gathered objects and information and recorded our impressions on camera.

The Capital of Culture competition proposes a clear link between the arts and the social and economic regeneration of our post-industrial cities. Then Culture Secretary Chris Smith said (of Glasgow, the UK's previous title holder, 1990) that the city experienced 'substantial economic and social benefits and made excellent use of arts and culture to strengthen and communicate its regeneration (European Capital of Culture). Cultural policy and the creative industries became the object of government attention during the re-branding of the Labour party into New Labour. Cultural policy and the creative industries were central to the mythology that was 'Cool Britannia', an image of the UK that would be spun around the world. Taking the lead from capital interests government hoped cultural industries would give post-industrial Britain new economic solutions to the tough complexities of advanced capitalism. Since taking power, the government has found that it has fewer options for economic intervention and they now seek to harness the magic of 'creativity' for their regeneration priorities of economic development and social improvement.

Culture remains the buzzword or 'get out of jail card' for our post-industrial cities. Culture has added value in the re-branding and marketing of the city as a centre for tourism and leisure. Highbrow or popular, culture is paraded as a symbol of a sophisticated and confident city: the arts are cool as they have the whiff of an intelligent, savvy and upwardly mobile culture. However with all UK cities now embarking on cultural reinvention in a fight for business and development opportunities (regardless of the Capital of Culture), it has become a competitive business in which to keep ahead.

The Capital of Culture 2008 is itself a cultural phenomenon, being the largest example of a culture-led regeneration competition. It offers the winning city a marketing windfall that promises to generate economic growth, inward investment and tourist cash, as well as a bonus for local politicians. Competing cities enter into a marketing war, like medieval city states in a free market jousting competition, draped in garish banners emblazoned with 'can do' slogans.

This form of competition can be useful when it tests the city and asks tough questions of its leaders and citizens. If the city is fully committed to developing a meaningful strategy it can become a tool with which to think about the future and one that can help generate initiatives. If it provides an opportunity for many more people to become involved with a vision of their city, it may offer new possibilities for a sense of civic society. It was the question of how these strategies were being developed that we took with us to the twelve competing cities.

We met with council officers and visual arts workers who gave us mixed views about the value of their cities bid. We found that in some cases the bid was used to develop long-term strategies and relationships that would improve the communication between community initiatives and the city council. But in the majority of cases there was concern that the bid team (often consultancy firms from outside the city) were not listening to those people at the grass roots of city culture, that their concerns were being bypassed or they were simply not part of the consultation process. The quality and relevance of some bid documents was clearly in question, perhaps the result of hasty decision-making processes. The common message to interested community groups was 'if we win, we can talk then'.

In our final analysis we hoped that when the marketing teams had gone home and the banners had come down, it would not all have been in vain. That the publicity material, printed brochures and hackneyed slogans ('Bristol is the best city in the world') generated through the process had not been made at the expense of existing funding for local services and cultural initiatives.

From the mass of collected images, brochures and badges we developed a work to present at the Independent at the Liverpool Biennial. The Liverpool Biennial was part of the art strategy for Liverpool's bid to become Capital of Culture 2008. The city of Liverpool and development partners funded the event in order to establish an international arts programme that would bring kudos to the city. The Independent section of the Biennial was an event proposed by groups working within the city, an event that would include city artists and local audiences. At the last minute the city council pulled the funding from this part of the Biennial. (North West Arts and the A Foundation had to step in to fund it, leaving it cash short). Artists in the city pointed to this lack of support for grass roots initiatives in favour of international projects as revealing the bigger agenda for culture in Liverpool. This context appeared to us the appropriate setting in which to present the outcome of the project.

The work WINNER comprised an image of the council chamber of each of the cities competing for CC2008. Each image was marked with the betting odds as provided by the bookmakers William Hill Ltd. The twelve poster-sized images were presented at St. Johns Market, a former food hall in the city centre.

The city council chamber represents the headquarters for political discourse, grand symbolic architecture, proudly decorated to depict the economic and political ambition of its ruling elite. The buildings are often nineteenth century, pointing to a period of growth and prosperity when the city fathers were powerful and held economic control of the city and the fortunes of its citizens.

The council chamber now stands as a symbol of an earlier imperial system of democracy. The power to affect 'local' economic, political or social change has been consumed by global conditions; local government is now an agency for regeneration and engaged in winning funding. The city council chamber still functions and but is now increasingly popular with tourists who may visit while following the city's heritage trail.

The Devonshire Quarter

We live and practice in Sheffield hence we take an active interest in the cultural policy of our adopted city. In 2001 we agreed to work with the planning department of the city council to develop a vision for the Devonshire Quarter area of the city. This experience was important in developing our understanding of the relationship between cultural policy and regeneration in the city.

Two of our recent projects, Outside Artspace and Showflat, highlight the contradictory relationship between public or democratic concerns and the interest of private property developers. The projects led us to question the City Council's ability to grasp and implement its own policy initiatives, in terms of design and planning, when dealing with private developers. Evidence of recent 'public art' within the city shows a spate of poorly conceived and executed projects. 'Art' is presented as decorative additions to cover poor and cheap building design and co-opted to provide ornamental security gates for new apartments block. Below we discuss the two projects with reference to some of the broader contexts, notably gentrification and how art and culture feature within the gentrification of the inner city.

Both projects took place in the Devonshire Quarter area of Sheffield. The Devonshire Quarter, now branded as 'DQ', has come to represent an exciting and youth-orientated space. The streets are home to small independent businesses selling life style and youth products. There are record shops, bars and cafes. Skateboarders hang out around the skateboard park and it is home to a growing student population, being in close proximity to the two universities. The development of large-scale student halls of residence in the vicinity has turned the area into a student village. The Devonshire Quarter has as its focus, Devonshire Green the only green space in the city centre.

The Devonshire Quarter has experienced widespread redevelopment. Sheffield, like most UK cities, is undergoing a boom in inner city development. People are moving back into the city centre, attracted by new apartment developments that offer a base for an urban life style. In his book *The New Urban Frontier*, Neil Smith outlines 'Gentrification as a structural product of the land and housing markets. Capital flows where the rate of return is highest, and the movement of capital to the suburbs, along with the continual de-valorization of inner-city capital, eventually produces the rent gap. When this gap grows sufficiently large rehabilitation (or for that matter, redevelopment) can begin to challenge the rates of return available elsewhere, and capital flows back in. Gentrification is a back to the city movement all right, but a back to the city movement by capital rather than people' (Smith, 1996).

Much of the Devonshire Quarter had remained undeveloped for many years. Areas within it, including Devonshire Green, had been neglected, seemingly awaiting transformation via a deal with investment capital. This lack of any remedial action prior to development of an area can be a tactic in itself. Rosalyn Deutsche and Cara Gendal Ryan state that this type of tactic was used to gentrify Lower East Side Manhattan,

> The first of these [tactics] is to do nothing at all, to allow the neighborhood to deteriorate of its own accord. Through a strategy of urban neglect, the city has been biding its time until enough contiguous lots can be put together to form sums of money at municipal auctions to developers who thus amass entire blocks for the construction of large-scale upper income housing (Deutsche and Ryan, 1984: 91–111).

The gentrification process reflects the desire by the middle class to impose cultural values and structure on urban surroundings. Improvements to the urban space through cultural policy including visual arts and urban design herald the changing culture of a site. Art and culture are tools within this gentrification of the inner city. The intervention of visual adornments within an urban design process symbolises a new middle class sophistication and can be marketed as such to potential investors. Art is co-opted by the city and by capital into this process.

The arts are also used to build bridges with existing communities, projects aiming to offer educational benefits and to reduce the number of those that feel excluded. 'From neighbourhood renewal to health, and from criminal justice system to employment, the arts has something to offer' (Arts and Social Policy). The function here for artists is to use participation and education to provide *innovative solutions* to 'worrying underclass behaviour'.

Outside Artspace

As lead artists we were asked to develop a vision for the Devonshire Quarter during ten days of research. The project was part of the SCC framework to regenerate the area, a private and public investment plan that would 'reinforce the identity of the area and improve land use, transport, urban design, the local economy, housing mix, sustainable living, quality of the environment and community safety'. Art and design were to have a key role in the regeneration strategy, 'acting as a focus for diverse ethnic and cultural activity and helping to develop a sense of the unique and vibrant identity of the Quarter'. The project was to consider the 16–24 age group as a main audience for the project, including the significant student population. The project was to establish an urban design directive for the development of Devonshire Green.

A large-scale apartment block development named West One was due to be built on one edge of the Devonshire Green. The apartments were marketed as exclusive. The development stood in a prime location, its eight stories benefiting from an unhindered view across the Devonshire Green. As part of these negotiations, Sheffield City Council asked the developer to provide '106 monies', a method commonly used by councils to enable funding for the improvements of green space and which can also include the funding of art works/projects. In the case of the Devonshire Quarter redevelopment, some of the 106 monies was to be used in order to fund our artists' research.

The developer's contribution via 106 was in our view not enough in relation to the advantage of winning planning permission for such a high building in a prime location. The new building was in no way sensitive to the surroundings and overshadowed the public green space. Our sentiments were shared by some council officers and it was questioned whether enough 106 money had been secured. The developer would also gain directly from any contribution to improvements made to the Green. We do not know how those interests might have impinged on the design process for the Green, as we were not party to any negotiations between the developer and council. We can only hope that the public interest within this 'third way' regeneration is strongly articulated.

Outside Artspace, West One and Devonshire Green, Hewitt and Jordan, 2002

During our research for the work Outside Artspace we visited the West One show room where we were told of the vision and future development of Devonshire Green. The sales team explained that the council planned to build a bandstand and make it very pleasant and safe, CCTV cameras would add further security. This misinformation; left any potential investor reassured by a vision of a recreation space made with them in mind just outside their apartment complex and clashed with our brief for an 16–24 audience. The sales team left us in no doubt that a key selling feature for West One was its views over and close proximity to the Green. Although the Green was a public space it was seen as an extension of the West One development, 'a front garden' feature for its occupants.

We worked directly with planning officers who had begun work on outlining the physical problems of the site. Before we could arrive at a vision, we needed to establish the function of the Green. The Green is very public space, with no restrictions on access (no gates, closing time, etc.), and the public it attracts is very diverse. In the summer months it is popular with children, city workers and shoppers. The space is also home to a considerable youth population centered on the skate park. It has few physical amenities with only simple bench seating and an informal area of trees; the topography gives the space a natural auditorium with a large grass area used for ball games and occasional outdoor events or festivals.

Our aim was to develop the green as an active 'social and public space' for a wide range of publics, therefore any physical improvements to the space would have to reflect this intention. We were aware of the gentrification agenda in the area but were intent on developing a project that re-energised the Green and that would encourage new uses and users within this public space. This was not a static garden space to be looked at; instead our aim was to maintain the sense of freedom in this space and to improve the access to it and the quality of its urban design.

Outside Artspace was our proposed work and revised function for Devonshire Green. The proposal outlined the space as a venue for art projects, exhibition, film, performance and interventions within an annual programme. The urban design of the space would be developed to support this. The arts and leisure would become a focus within the space alongside an improved green space. There would be facilities for music events and a new play area for children.

We discussed this idea with a number of artists groups, agencies, commissioners and community groups in the city in order to test its feasibility. All the groups consulted overwhelmingly supported the proposal and stated as part of the consultation document that they would wish to contribute to the programme. Those questioned said it would offer a much-needed public event space in the city centre. The very public nature of the space appealed to others and the provision of systems to enable the presentation of various form of media was seen as a positive way of establishing a hub of activity where there had previously been none.

The consultation with prospective partners was a positive outcome of the project. It highlighted the need for further cross group collaborations and revealed the shared desire to develop strategies and policy that would improve the representation of the arts in the city. This initiative was particularly important, as many believed the city was not effectively meeting its cultural potential and they questioned the city council's commitment to its cultural policy.

At the end of our research (April 2002) our contribution was received and our contact with the council abruptly stopped. The recommendations we made have not been taken up. We have had reports that the council has returned to an original design idea: to improve the design of the site and visually enrich it with Gaudi-inspired tiling design. The gentrification of the Devonshire Green goes on. We watch with interest to see what the priorities are for the space and who the beneficiaries are.

While working on Outside Artspace we played a major part in developing a Regional Lottery Arts Programme application to the Arts Council for S1 Artspace. Our proposal was to develop a series of five art projects both off site and at S1 Artspace. This application was informed by our proposal for Outside Artspace. We were successful with the application and S1 Artspace were able to appoint a co-coordinator, Michelle Cotton, to carry out and develop these projects further. 'Alternative Action Plan' was the first project to go ahead in November 2003. This saw five artists make new work for the area around the Devonshire Green.

The SHOWFLAT Project

More recently, space itself has begun to be bought and sold. Not the earth, the soil, but social space, produced as such, with this purpose, this finality (so to speak). Space is no longer only an indifferent medium, the sum of places where surplus value is created, realized, and distributed. It becomes the product of social labour, the very general object of production, and consequently of the formation of surplus value" (Lefebvre, 2003: 154)

In 2003 we made SHOW FLAT, a project commissioned as part of the city-wide arts festival Artsheffield 03. Our experience of developing the Outside Artspace project had led us to consider the relationship between art practice and gentrification. By proposing the SHOWFLAT project we aimed to further examine 'culture-led' regeneration.

Our studio space at S1 Artspace is situated within the Devonshire Quarter as outlined above. The increase in real estate value in the area has begun to push the previously eclectic mix of light industry and cultural activity out of the Devonshire Quarter. Ironically, but not for the first time, the community that made it a magnet for inward investment now could not afford to stay, despite a strategy document developed by the planning department (Devonshire Quarter Action Plan) that promoted a vision of the two communities co-existing. The area has urban chic and this is a valuable commodity for developers. Our studio is now surrounded by new and redeveloped buildings for student accommodation and 'city living' apartment blocks. It is unclear how long we will be able to comfortably operate within this context.

SHOWFLAT, Exterior signage, Hewitt and Jordan, 2003

In SHOW FLAT we decided to pre-empt the inevitable redevelopment of our site by real estate speculators by doing it ourselves. We developed our studio office into a small two-roomed apartment with fine views towards Devonshire Green, the heart of the Devonshire Quarter that offers a 'unique opportunity for a new adventure in urban living' (Sales brochure). SHOW FLAT exhibits the current interior design languages so essential for city living: white walls to reflect light, wood laminate floors, minimal decoration and modern door furniture.

We did not wish to present our studio as the final barricade against the forces of capital. Doing so may suggest that the studio is a special or spiritual space for art practice, a nostalgic or modernist view that we are definitely opposed to. As we choose to operate within the public realm we are not dependent upon studio space; the studio is a project space for experimentation and discussion. We are, however, concerned by the power of capital and its influence on the shaping of public or democratic processes in the city. Our studio on this occasion became a tool with which we could discuss these issues.

Cultural policy can be divisive. Culture-led regeneration is only representative of a wider constituency and culture of the city when it is developed alongside a social policy stemming from a vigorous and democratic political process. This demands a political system that has the confidence to take on and discuss the bigger and longer-term problems affecting the city. We began to see SCC cultural policy as being complicit with the process of gentrification.

The foundations for a new urbanism will not come from market driven redevelopment policies that present exclusive apartment buildings as a model of progress. The growing influence of private development can bring wealth to a city but requires firm negotiation to bring down the best possible deal for the wider community. (Can the council play poker?) The city is currently immersed in plans for exclusive apartments but there are very few social housing developments, so anyone with less capital will be dependent upon that older model of redevelopment called the 'trickle down effect'. This divergent trend in the prosperity of the inhabitants of our cities is a significant cultural feature that goes unmentioned within cultural policy documents.

Ironically, artists can also be the victims of their own success. Tim Butler and Garry Robson in their book London Calling point to the gentrification in East London and the 'artists quarter' in London Fields boosted by Hackney's attempt to encourage the creative industries. 'The role the artists have played (unwittingly) in gentrification elsewhere suggests they are more subtle shock troops than the Slug and Lettuce but in other respects are more effective and formidable in marking change. Already it is said that many artists are moving out of London Fields as they are unable to afford the rents when leases come up for renewal' (Butler and Robson, 2003: 180).

How unwitting this is we find questionable. Artists are often from middle class backgrounds and can aim to effect the redevelopment of an area through their desire to live in a location and engage with its specific urban conditions, to change it to something they find preferable. While their incomes may not be high, their life style aspirations can be the same as other middle class professionals.

SHOWFLAT, Interior, Hewitt and Jordan, 2003

Bibliography

Arts and Social Policy Statement. Department of Culture, Media and Sport website. <www.culture.gov.uk>

Butler, T. with Robson, G. (2003) *London Calling: The Middle Classes and the Remaking of Inner London.* Oxford; Berg.

European Capital of Culture. Foreword by the Secretary of State for Culture, Media and Sport. Department of Culture, Media and Sport website. <www.culture.gov.uk>

Lefebvre, H. (2003) *The Urban Revolution.* Translated by R. Bononno. Foreword by Neil Smith. Minneapolis: University of Minnesota Press.

Negri, A. and Hardt, M. (1997) *Die Arbeit des Dionysos, Materialististische Staatskritik in de Postmoderne.* Berlin: [ed: publisher?].

Smith, N. (1996) *The New Urban Frontier: Gentrification and the Revanchist City.* London: Routledge.

West.one Sheffield Sales brochure.

Laima Kreivyte

Going Public: Strategies of Intervention in Lithuania

This essay examines the development of contemporary public art in relation to a range of sites and social practices in post-1989 Lithuania. It asks how different artistic interventions in urban sites influenced the production of space during the political changes of the time and how ideologically constructed public space (expressed by a powerful verticality in Soviet monuments) was substituted by consumerist space (emphasizing horizontality and flatness of the surface, expressed in advertisements). It asks, too, what was the role of the artist and the community in producing a more dynamic form of the public discourse.

Lithuania in the 1990s saw an expansion of institutional and alternative art practices. This was closely related to the political/social process of *perestroika*, especially the struggle for freedom of speech and, consequently, artistic expression. We can distinguish two types of artistic interventions in public places: sculptural and performative. The sculptural approach stemmed from sculpture symposiums − a frequent occurrence in the old East bloc countries − and developed to site-specific art projects in the city. Place and context were the most important factors for sculptural interventions. Artists and curators explored and appropriated old houses, abandoned factories, shop windows, streets and flats. While the sculptural approach emphasized site and representation, the performative one drew attention to time and participation. Site-specific projects and installations which addressed different social groups mostly as viewers and archaeologists (or 'space explorers'), temporary art events, happenings and performances encouraged greater participation and communication - though the artistic strategies of intervention were more varied than this simple scheme suggests. During the past decade, the majority of public art projects addressed both temporality and site-specificity, looking for a shared space of experience.

Entering the Public Realm: the (Post) Totalitarian Shock

During the 90s artists tried to avoid the official norms and ideological requirements of making art and tested their approaches by making works for hitherto (and to an extent still) strictly regulated public spaces. The first successful attempt to reconfigure an industrial public space was the Symposium of Concrete Sculpture, organized by Mindaugas Navakas (b. 1952) in the Large Block Factory in Vilnius in 1985. The sculptures were exhibited in the industrial environment of the factory near a railroad connecting the capital, Vilnius, and Kaunas City. At the time, this event was described as bridging the gap between nature and civilization. In fact it marked the birth of industrial urban sculpture which owing, to its material, scale and architectural appearance established a new relationship with public space. Concrete sculpture became an alternative model both to public monuments (as ideological and architectural implements of the state's power) and to decorative sculptural accents produced for recreational zones.

One of the key figures of the transitional period was Mindaugas Navakas, who subverted old notions of sculpture and monumentality. His way of interacting with the public was based on creating a shock-experience, an interruption of normal perceptions and codes. As a result of the technologies and materials he deployed (concrete was followed by rusted steel, asbestos cement and silicone afterwards), the rhetoric of power became a key issue in Navakas's public sculptures. His artistic tactics are reminiscent of a viral attack: huge and aggressive sculptures attack the building, take control over it and establish new types of subordination – which critically re-frame the old subordinations. Public space is for Navakas a site for the power games of contesting ideologies, where even architecture and sculpture are struggling for survival. We can find traces of paradoxical thinking, employing contradictory juxtapositions of sculpture and architecture in Navakas's zincographs from *Vilnius Notebook* (1986, the first solo exhibition of Navakas in the House of Architects, Vilnius). In these pictures one can see enormous sculptures confronting the most famous buildings of the city: the Opera and Ballet Theatre, the Hotel Lietuva, and the chimneys of Gariunai market place. Sudden enlargement and changing proportions sometime produce a comic effect but only to the point where representation meets reality. Conceptual sculpture (as critics used to call zincographs), produced in actual public space generates a potential discourse of social critique. *The Hook* (1994) is attached to the front of a Stalinist façade in place of the Soviet State emblem; the sculpture resembles one of its basic elements – the sickle – turned upside down. To paraphrase Douglas Crimp's observation about Richard Serra's *Tilted Arc*, Navakas' hook metaphorically ruptures the spatial expression of state power by destroying its symbols and the building's coherence (see Crimp, 1993: 176). *Three Large Reliant Sculptures* exhibited in front of the Contemporary Art Centre in Vilnius addresses the issue of the museum's role in contemporary consumerist society and, on the other hand, ironically refers to the prevalent institutional hunger for the big names in the largest exhibition place in Lithuania. The iron irony, so to speak, of Navakas's work is meant to deconstruct the supposed heroic gesture of *The Artist* (as either totalitarian state servant or romantic genius) and to provoke a critical response in the passer-by. Navakas creates counter-monuments – large, aggressive and at the same time enchained forms which in many cases need a prop found in the built environment – be it a wall or a building. It is not a case of the freestanding, elevated statue in the middle of a square; more a barricade in front of the main entrance, frightening through its potential instability. Diagonals break ideal verticality and the aggressive form is pressed to the site with the power of several tons.

Critical intervention, site-specificity/contextual dependence, large scale and rough industrial material became, then, important features of public art in Lithuania at the end of 1980s and beginning of 1990s.

Mindaugas Navakas, *The Hook,* 1994

Collective Actions: From Philosophical Ideas to Political and Social Issues

Public art is not a homogeneous entity with clear linear development from experimental decorative sculpture in the open-air to industrial site specific projects and urban interventions. Sculptural activities mark only one thread in this complex scheme of public interactions. Public art, as we see it now, is a complex network of interactions: of an artist and the community, an artwork and the specific site, the cultural environment and public response. Therefore it is necessary to discuss new artistic strategies which emerged after the political and cultural changes of the 1990s.

With the re-establishment of Lithuanian independence – which is both a revival of nationalism after the Russian period and a post-communism – the postmodern influences of cultural discourses in the West began to affect cultural debate in Lithuania. After the dismantling of the Berlin Wall in 1989, all available information channels and travelling experiences were deployed to fill the gap left by a kind of cultural amnesia bred by isolation – in a very short time lessons and examples of conceptual art, minimalism, land art, site-specific projects, actions and installations were implemented and legitimised. The cultural climate was extremely friendly for all kinds of changes and innovations. One of the characteristic features of this period was a turn to collective or collaborative art projects. Artists began to form different groups according to their own interests: for instance, *Zalias lapas* (Green Leaf) in Vilnius and *Post-Ars* in Kaunas, both established in 1990.

Action Road by Zalias lapas (Gedimnas Urbonas, Dziugas Katinas, Aidas Bareikis, Julius Ludavicius, Arturas Makstutis, Gintaras Sodeika, etc.) happened on 12 October , 1990 – International Day of Human Rights. Black and white human figures made of chalk and soot in the street in front of the Town Hall were scattered by passers-by and cars through the entire Old Town. The audience became active participants in creating the meaning of the work. The group issued a manifesto, saying that an important feature of their action was to involve 'a car driver as art creator and consumer'. Other actions and performances by Zalias lapas were also inspired by philosophical observations about the human condition in a changing society and often addressed issues of temporality and the artist's body.

Post-Ars (Aleksas Andriuskevicius, Robertas Antinis Junior and Ceslovas Lukenskas) is well-known for its complex actions in specific places, such as quarry Zatysiai, where different performances and events takes place simultaneously. *Covering Surface* by Antinis can be seen as a negative projection of the human body, which is literally brought to earth and covered. The glorious verticality of the human figure as a sign of reason and dignity – *Homo erectus* – is replaced by a total passivity and anonymity, emphasizing the temporality of its being. An interesting play of verticals and horizontals as well as rhythmic construction of space as a sound system was presented in the installation in open space *Score II* by Post-Ars in Niederlausitz, Germany.

Crossing the street: Public Art as Meeting Place

What does it mean for the art to go into the street? The question is not new. What street? The one described rather nostalgically by Lewis Mumford (1961) as one of the basic structural elements of the city? Or the place in which outsiders wander (and wonder), as for Baudelaire's flaneur? Or maybe the street of a contemporary city, described by Richard Sennett as an 'area to move through, not to be in' (Sennett (1974) cited in Bauman, 1994: 158)? For the most part, for artists the street means an open space outside the gallery. Despite different contexts and multicultural everyday encounters, this understanding of the street is just, I would argue, a shadow of the museum, or its negative projection. To go to the street for Art_ras Raila means first of all to meet all the people who use it – not to show art to strangers and test their reactions (like widening access to art) but to invite different (mostly sub-cultural) groups to participate in the production of an art project by presenting their attitudes and activity to themselves and others. A rave club, a rap group, bikers, professional dancers, members of an illegal political party, a provincial hard rock group and others took part in various art projects in public places. They were not represented as exotic curiosities or the stereotypical Other invited for fun by a gifted trainer. Far from it – the artist was a mediator between the so-called art world and a range of publics. This process is demonstrated in Raila's performance Pump for Art – Art for Pump within the public art project Mundane Language (3rd Exhibition, the Soros Center for Contemporary Arts – Lithuania, Vilnius, 1995). A small, empty Vilnius city square served as a stage for the performance of the RAVE Club and RAP Group. According to Rail, 'the participants serve as art for themselves, they are void of any memory, and the site specificity presents no importance for them' (Lankelis, 1996: 37).

Raila understands public art as social interaction or artistic intervention in different communities. The collective process of art production and consumption characterizes his rejection of the normative distinction between public and private realms. As Lucy Lippard (1990) puts it, 'Public art is accessible art of any kind, that cares about/ challenges/involves and consults the audience for or with whom it is made, respecting community and environment. The other stuff is still private art, no matter how big or exposed or intrusive it might be. Despite a declared openness and nonhierarchical politic, today, most art institutions remain a closed circle of well-established professionals – artists, critics, curators. Raila is constantly breaking the system by insisting on hybridity as a cultural tactic. During the international performance festival Dimension O in Vilnius in 1997, Raila invited a bikers' club called Crazy in the Dark to ride their motorcycles through the Contemporary Art Center. One by one, bikers crossed the entrance and the main hall, moved through the courtyard and reached the street. The action was repeated in order to make a live circle of motorcyclists crossing the borders of the city's main contemporary art institution and the streets outside it. The official art space was penetrated by powerful street culture. At the same time, bikers enjoyed their new role as active participants in artistic practice. When I asked the author what was the most important outcome of this performance, Raila said, 'Bikers from Crazy in the Dark found out where the Contemporary Art Centre is'.

Extensions of the Body

Arturas Raila perceives city as a meeting place. Egle Rakauskaite experiences the city as

Egle Rakauskaite, *Trap: Expulsion from Paradise.* 1995

an extension of a person, as her/his clothes, to borrow an expression from Marshall McLuhan (1994). Her actions and installations addressed temporality (both in an technological and ontological sense), gender issues and power relations represented by symbolic order and revealing painful experiences. In her installation Net, two abandoned houses in the former territory of the Vilnius ghetto were connected over the street by a net made from human hair. Hair in Raila's works functioned not only as abject material but also (more often) as a powerful representation of the disciplined body of a social constraining situation. An especially manifold approach to the female body was demonstrated in the live sculpture *Trap: Expulsion from Paradise* (1995), probably the most famous work by Rakauskait to date, shown in Vilnius and staged later in Warsaw, Istanbul, Zagreb, Stockholm and Athens. Thirteen young girls in white dresses were connected by their braids to a strong and seemingly unbreakable live grid, threatening in its silent stillness. The work created an impression of observing, as if with a microscope, an extremely enlarged molecular structure of patriarchal society – a structure which survived through centuries and was installed, as it were, in women's bodies and dressing codes. The author comments that her work emphasizes the corporeal dimension and the influence of the normative context on our perception / reception of the body:

> I would rather have *Trap: Expulsion from Paradise* viewed as an image of the young body: indistinct, indistinguishable from other young bodies, and yet so alive. I want the work – the girls, the costumes, the setting – to look as generalized as possible. Then it comes to life (Jablonskien and Schafhausen, 2002: 128).

In her later performances Rakauskaite continued exploration of the social and mythical dimensions of the body. Organic materials (honey, fat, chocolate) refer both to consumption (food) and decay (temporality) and at the same time question the naturalness of the female body. In the middle of the 1990s, however, consumerist ideology became one of the main targets for artists working in social space.

Mundane Language of Consumerism

In 1995 the site-specific project *For Yourself and Others* (curated by Liutauras Psibilskis) took place in department stores, cafes and similar places. A huge fur mammoth with a tusk was installed in a shop window and paintings in the classical style (designating the mimetic tradition) were displayed above the counter along with the usual meat and sausages and a minimalist cube of glass test-tubes with fake blood samples was placed in the pharmacy. People from the street were encouraged to consume artworks together with commodities. The participants did not simply confront consumerist ideology but compared its stereotypes with soviet and nationalist ones – themselves quite different. For example, Academic Training Group (Giedrius Kumetaitis, Mindaugas Ratavicius) presented a project entitled *Fluxus genies* – two TV screens with static images of two classmates, who later became famous – the 'fluxus pope' George Maciunas and Vytautas Landsbergis, the chairmen of the Lithuanian Parliament. By making this comparison the artists presented the ruling of the country as a continuation of a fluxus project.

Gediminas Urbonas, *Coming or Going*, 1995

The same year, another public art project took place in the old town of Vilnius. As the title *Mundane Language* suggests, the main strategy of the curator Algis Lankelis was to establish a dialogue between art practice and everyday life. Some artists chose to transform the elements of the surrounding architecture and to challenge perceptions of the city, while others focused their attention on social and political issues. Sculpture in many cases functioned as a cultural reference, a meeting point of past and present. Gediminas Urbonas covered the heads of bronze sculptures from the soviet period with mirror cubes and entered the debate about the future of these statues. The sculptures of soviet working people and soldiers were placed on the bridge – so the passer-by could observe the flow of the river and clouds on the mirror surface. One could read it as a simple message: sculpture mirrors its time and society, which is changing all the time. This work inspired a heated debate in the cultural and daily press and on television. It is one of the best examples of how public art in general and sculpture in particular has moved from the representational to the discursive, through its move into public space.

Mobile Cells of the Society: Shared Space of 'Nomadic' Experience

Contemporary public art takes place not only in shared physical but also in virtual space. Yet, according to my experience placing an ad in the newspaper and on the Internet, we still feel more comfortable in Gutenberg's galaxy than in the global village of new technologies. In order to address more people in Lithuania, it is better to go to the biggest daily paper. And the equivalent of the linear and hierarchical structure of a newspaper in the realm of public transport is a trolley bus.

The public art project *Identification* in Vilnius City trolley buses (September 1999) was organized with the intention of reaching those people who usually do not go to contemporary art exhibitions. There were only 20 trolley buses involved in the project out of 300 in use in the city – it was quite a difficult task to see everything in one week. But art professionals were not the main target group. Entering public transport meant an encounter with an unprepared as well as heterogeneous public. As Malcolm Miles notes in a chapter on art in metropolitan public transport in *Art, Space and the City*, 'mass transit systems are locations of more informal mixing in urban society than almost anywhere else' (Miles, 1997: 144). To elicit a direct response, the artist-participants in the project not only changed the interior space of vehicles, but also travelled with 'their' trolley buses themselves – commenting on their works, engaging in the discussions, documenting the reactions of users. A trolley bus is a mini model of society: a driver, passengers representing different groups travelling together the same way but with different intentions. And then you have a strict and stubborn system of control – to remember that we still live in post-soviet times.

Metaphorically, the trolley bus is a mobile cell of post-soviet society. You can enter and exit wherever you want but only at bus stops. You have to follow the schedule and you cannot change the route. The aim of artistic intervention was to merge the collective experience of travelling with that of art, to transform a means of transportation into one of intense communication, to disturb the daily routine of mundane life. It was a challenge not only to users but also to the artists.

Kostas Bogdanas (1961) opted to express his ideas about art in public transport by doing something useful – he cleaned one trolley bus every morning during the project. Instead of a visually attractive installation the artist placed a simple message inside:

> Dear Passengers,
> Sometimes (to be honest – very often) I doubt the importance of art/artist in the society. Probably a clean and tidy trolley bus is more needed by common people than art. I wash and clean this trolley bus every day this week.
> K.Bogdanas (artist)

Other artists decided to decorate the interior, to offer more individuality and comfort to passengers. In most cases a decorative approach was deployed not to please the gaze but rather to activate tactile perception or to mask a subversive message. White pillows on the seats or rose laces on the handles signalled the intrusion of privacy into the public realm, for example. Suddenly the trolley bus became a mere decoration, like something in a soap opera, and the passengers started to behave accordingly. If the transformation of the setting produced a more relaxed atmosphere, the direct encounter with the artist was in a way mobilising and sometimes stressful. It was interesting to observe the responses of the audience during the performance *Sanitary Day*. Three girls (Aida Kacinskaite, Inga Raubaite and Vilma Sileikiene) dressed in white doctors' smocks caps and sunglasses entered the trolley bus and started to wash the handles, pretending that they were doing sanitary cleaning. Many people took this action for real, not as artistic activity. A man with a broken nose asked them to bandage his wound. Interestingly, the ticket collector was very supportive – she took the side of the artists against the passengers, although artists themselves didn't feel it was a confrontation. According to the performers, public responses (both positive and negative) to their work tended to depend on a few people, who loudly voiced their feelings about what was going on. Others tended to agree with them, while old people expressed gratitude on behalf of all the passengers.

The above presents a selective view of some twenty years of public art in Lithuania, with attention to the most important and interactive cases, as I see them. Artists, this view shows, have employed different strategies of interaction with social spaces. First they tried to conquer the city (Navakas), then to appropriate it (site-specific projects), then to move through it and communicate with its publics (art in trolley buses). Public art projects moved slowly from representation to information; on the way, were engagements not only with passive bodies but also active participants and groups from different parts of society. Rosalind Krauss (1983) argued that sculpture in the expanded field is neither land nor architecture. To continue thinking in that direction we can conclude that contemporary public art is a social practice based on various strategies of interaction; it crosses the boundaries between inside and outside, private and public, the street and the art institution. Future strategies will open even more possibilities for creative cultural hybridity.

Bibliography

Baudelaire, C. (1964) *The painter of Modern life and Other Essays.* London: Phaidon

Bauman, Z. (1994) *Postmodern Ethics.* London: Blackwell.

Crimp, D. (1993) *On the Museum's Ruins.* Cambridge: MIT Press.

Foster, H., ed. (1983) *The Anti-Aesthetic: essays on postmodern culture.* Seattle: Bay Press.

Jablonskiene, L. and Schafhausen, N. (eds) (2002) *Changing Society: Lithuania.* New York: Lucas & Sternberg.

Krauss, R. (1983) 'Sculpture in the Expanded Field', in Foster (1983) pp. 31-42.

Lankelis, A. (ed) (1996) *Mundane Language.* Vilnius: Soros Center for Contemporary Arts - Lithuania.

Lippard, L. (1990) 'Mixed Blessings: New Art in a Multicultural America'. New York: Pantheon .

McLuhan, M. (1994) *Understanding Media: The Extensions of Man.* Cambridge, MA: The MIT Press.

Miles, M. (1997) *Art, Space and the City: Public art and Urban Future.* London: Routledge.

Mumford, L. (1961) *The City in History: Its Origins, its Transformations, and its Prospects.* Harmondsworth: Penguin Books.

Introduction

A burgeoning confidence (at least in some parts) that what artists do can have 'real' effects, i.e. material, measurable, reportable (beneficial), seems to be afoot. A number of institutionally supported public art projects fit this paradigm; providing opportunities for artists to do something 'good', like melt guns, or clean a river, or open up a new public space. Of course this causes suspicion and, for me, even a certain deflation. The world is organized to encourage and respond to results-oriented thinking and to reward creativity as long as it is lassoed towards productivity in a limited and measurable sense. One of the liabilities of doing work that attempts to initiate environmental or social change is the likelihood of it being seen only in limited terms – reduced to its short-term and material goals, eclipsing its symbolic critique. Another is that the mechanisms involved in pursuing a clearly defined goal will foreclose the open process that I have always valued as a critical factor in art-making (as well as in long-term social change). To what degree do we compromise potential non-measurable effects (changes in values and thought structures) in our ambition and 'seriousness' to affect policy, our eagerness to engage with structures of institutional support and our determination to inscribe real effects in real terms?

These questions can only be meaningfully addressed in relation to specific projects. The best construct multiple levels of interpretive access, such as Dan Peterman's Endless Table, a hundred foot picnic table made from the slightly sad material of extruded recycled plastic. The futility of significantly 'solving' the accumulating waste from our collective plastics consumption is glaringly evident in the seemingly endless potential extension of the table's repeated units, next to its actual limit of one hundred feet. But Chicago loved the table's immediate usefulness; people sat all along it at lunch hour, eating takeout food in plastic containers. Does this contradiction suggest failure or some version of art's capacity to, in Herbert Marcuse's words, "represent reality while accusing it"? For Marcuse, art provided a realm slightly offset from the pragmatic real, a realm in which what's missing from that real might be glimpsed .

Frankfurt School writers (Horkheimer, Adorno, Marcuse, et al.) developed understandings of the term instrumental that go beyond simply goal-oriented thinking and refer more specifically to what they saw as the effects of an increasingly automated and administered society, in which technology infiltrates as bureaucratized consciousness and transforms people and ideas into tools (instruments) employed to achieve a goal. Art on the other hand was held out as an opposite and antidote: valuing process, sensuous immersion in immediate experience, and 'things' in themselves. For these writers, the enlightenment project, in its pursuit of freedom, channelled all of life's energies into the routines of rationality. But according to Adorno, we ought to be able to enjoy both intention and immersion: why couldn't Odysseus dive into the sea when called by the sirens and revel in the sensuous experience of their song, as well as swim back to the boat later and continue on, towards home, and Penelope? The impossibility of imagining both exposes the fear behind the exercise of power: 'The self-dominant intellect … separates from sensuous experience in order to subjugate it.'

'Sensuous immersion' can also be understood as giving up a certain kind of control, especially in the context of collaboration. Between intention and effect is a gap in which a lot can happen. What I see as a problem of instrumentalism in some public art and community based projects is a problem of social relations, as well as loss of symbolic reach. Instrumental action often leads to authoritarian methods, since so much has to be suppressed to focus on the goal. This can be a problem if you are working with others, as well as if you are merely exercising authority over yourself. Tightening the logic of cause and effect linearises our actions and supposes a subject who is transparent to herself. But we are neither wholly rational selves, nor are our intentions ever perfectly mirrored in their effects. Working in open-ended ways allows the positive aspects of this uncontrollable situation to come through – responding inventively to contradiction, disruption and detour and the unpredictable contributions of collaborators. Acting instrumentally erases such complexities in order to get something done.

Projects

The following descriptions of three projects which I have worked on are presented not as prime or wholly successful examples but as attempts to reconcile intention with immersion in the form of open-ended processes. Collaboration plays a different role in each case. I hope that the descriptions convey the complex interactions that for me made the projects interesting.

Flood

The art collaborative Haha, of which I am a member (with Wendy Jacob, John Ploof, and until 1998, Richard House), built and operated a hydroponic garden in a storefront in Chicago for three years, between 1992 and 1995. The garden was initially sponsored for one year by Sculpture Chicago, a public art organization, and continued to operate for two additional years with private support and the participation of a group of between 12 and 35 people collectively called 'Flood'. The garden produced kale, collard and mustard greens that we gave to AIDS service organizations providing food to people with HIV/AIDS (meals on wheels and hospice programmes). Clients of these organizations received occasional bags of fresh greens with their hot food. We also served free weekly meals on site and grew herbs used as immune boosters and anticarcinogens. But the garden was less geared towards maximizing production and more towards creating a place for people to come to, framed by the need to address the sense of helplessness many of us felt in relation to the AIDS epidemic at the time. We

held weekly meetings and periodic public events, and anyone could drop in. It was an open proposition, actively functioning as a garden but also exploring how and in what ways its initial structure might be taken up and used (as opposed to our fully determining its use from the start).

Haha chose the extreme conditions of hydroponics – its sterile chemisty – initially as a symbolic precaution against the danger of opportunistic infections caused by microorganisms in dirt. This small control was not practically significant but the sterility and piping structure of the system suggested hospitals and western medicine (in contrast to the luxuriant greens close to harvest time). We also chose hydroponics for the image of interconnection (i.e. a voluntary community) that the system's plumbing provided – all the roots grew together in a tangled net. These levels of metaphor provided ways to read art in the project, for those who might be confused, though some in the mainstream media labelled the project 'social work' – meaning it had slipped into a different discipline and didn't qualify as art. It *was* social and it *was* work but part of what made it not 'social work' was that we had no single, definite, goal, other than to see what would happen. We could have tried to specify limited goals and outcomes in grant application style – so many school groups visited, so many video screenings, so many bags of greens delivered. But what we couldn't define or locate was Flood's fundamentally anomalous existence – not a school, not a clinic, not a store, not a factory – and no one drew a salary.

We did have 'results' – many local school groups visited the garden to talk about sex, AIDS, healthcare, science; an AIDS support group adopted the site for their own separate meetings; a fourteen year old who lived on the block came out as gay and positive and found his way to counselling and peer support. We sponsored lectures, learned about different kinds of treatments, collected and passed out tons of literature, as well as condoms. But while these concrete effects might establish a kind of legitimacy, they weren't what made the project worth the trouble. Instead, for me, it was Flood's unexpected relation to the street, its residents and businesses and also passers-by (it was a block away from a train stop). The undefinability of Flood's activity created a question that drew people in to talk. That undefinability also inspired conversations about needs and absences in city life: the desire for connection to the place you live and the people around you, as opposed to the anonymity so many felt; the need for adequate healthcare and for referrals and peer education so as not to have to be dependent on the experts; the need for public spaces that were warm; the need to ask questions about things you feel you should know and not feel stupid; and, more generally, the need for non-commercial and collective activities to be present and visible in the city, manifesting values not co-opted by someone else's intent to make a buck, or push their religion. These conversations seemed more significant to me than any other aspect of the project. Flood was a little of all of those things but none wholeheartedly, yet that very undefinability allowed visitors to articulate a range of unmet needs and imagine things differently than what already existed.

Choosing to follow through with any one of the potential directions generated by these conversations would have created a different project. When the garden dissolved, some of its members worked with local non-profits to create a new consortium of AIDS support agencies and social services nearby and donated the Flood hardware. The consortium hoped to use it as office window dressing – but it was too complicated to maintain and ended up in the basement. Flood's value (for me) was its perpetual potential, like an open door, and what this allowed people to see and imagine into, in order to come to their own solutions. A purposiveness is still assumed in this but it is indirect. I suppose I am talking about a utopian quality because when something is realized this quality disappears. Instrumental action remains inside the possible, and measurable, but what's possible and measurable remains partial because its potential has been removed. Not that Flood offered wholeness or completion – only an intimation of something more than what is here.

3 Acres on the Lake: DuSable Park Proposal Project

This project focused entirely on an imaginary realm of potential but also intersected with pragmatic Chicago politics in a curious way. I began the project in 2001 as an independently initiated call for proposals for how to use a piece of public land on the lakefront in downtown Chicago. There was no sponsorship and I had no authority to do this, just the question, what would you like to see here? – and the assumption that 'the public' (or publics) should have a say in the use of public land. The sixty-five proposals that came in were exhibited twice in Chicago as well as online (www.artic.edu/~apalme) and a catalogue was published through WhiteWalls, Inc. The proposals ranged in practicality from detailed bioremediation centres to a lesbian retirement home in the shape of a bathtub, and some reiterated the traditions of public art – flatten it and erect a shiny monument. My desire from the beginning was never to choose among them but to present all the proposals together as a version of collective potential, representing multiple publics and unconstrained by practicalities or preference (the one constraint was to maintain a commemoration to DuSable (see below). One of my main questions was how (and whether) the exhibition and publication might influence the trajectory of the land's actual development, without having to be sucked dry of its imaginative leaps by the deadening city politics inevitably involved in promoting any one specific proposal.

The lot was complicated: it had already been dedicated in 1987 to become a memorial park commemorating Jean Baptiste DuSable, a black explorer who founded the first non-indigenous permanent settlement in Chicago. With a change of city administrations (from black to white), the promise to develop a park dedicated to the memory of a black historical figure (also a colonist) had been entirely neglected. The lot also happened to be contaminated with radioactive thorium, though the extent of this contamination has never been definitively established. And, the lot is difficult to get to – jutting out from underneath a highway. I was initially drawn to it as an inaccessible, unkempt meadow in the heart of high-price real estate. I wasn't excited to see it developed as the promised park because all such parks end up looking exactly alike, destroying this anomalously bucolic sight. But I knew something would happen soon and without public pressure it would likely be commandeered by private interests.

I joined the coalition demanding that the city develop the park even though I didn't necessarily agree that a thirty-five foot bronze statue of DuSable was the ideal memorial. The proposal project and the coalition work aimed for different things and used different methods but also used each other in a way that allowed both instrumental and aesthetic efforts to remain distinct and uncompromised.

The coalition borrowed the proposal project for an exhibition to draw attention to the city's unkept promise and to generate popular support for their cause. Although initially suspicious, in the end neither the bathtub nor the school in the shape of an nineteenth century frigate run by retired romantic painters bothered them, since coalition members came to understand the speculative nature of the project and the value of its inclusiveness. The project has intercepted and changed the situation that provided its initial platform, while retaining a degree of the volatile virtual – or whatever you want to call it – a mote of potential unhampered by the logic of 'sense'. The park has yet to be developed – a steering committee has been appointed but no park district money set aside.

Taxi

Haha's current project uses a digital sign on top of a taxicab to distribute messages generated by local residents to specific locations in a city. The locations are defined by GPS coordinates which are linked to the message display. In Chicago, where we did a trial run in the spring of 2003, the seventy-five messages we received from email and direct solicitations of groups and schools ranged from anti-war (outside the Federal Building) to very personal ('hi Grandma Dot' outside her house). 'Just because it says 4 for $1 doesn't mean you have to buy 4' flashed in front of Dominick's, a mega-supermarket. Although Haha reserved the right to edit submissions, this wasn't necessary, perhaps because we had lots of pre-existing contacts in Chicago and the solicitation of messages was somewhat controlled (i.e. apparently no fundamentalist Christian or neo-Nazi groups heard about this opportunity). In North Adams, MA, where Haha will do another version of Taxi this spring, we don't have any pre-existing connections and are joining efforts with a local alliance of non-profits including religious groups. We don't know what we will get. This situation raises a different issue in relation to instrumentality. The 'purpose' of this project is in part to detourne an advertising technology from manipulating target audiences based on market research (cigarette ads outside high schools...) to providing a specifically local message system that residents can use for their own purposes. But what will they say? In all of these projects, and in valorizing potential as a precursor to change, the element of unpredictability keeps the results radically open. Just because people might be able to glimpse a future different from now doesn't mean they will choose the same one – or do something to make it happen.

In the context of an instrumentalized world, I look for work that presents a difficulty, that acts like a low-level stomach-ache – not acutely painful but systemically queasy. I expect it to be hard for it to 'fit in' and for it to encounter resistance from organized powers, because what it has to offer in the best sense is something other than what we already have or know. At the same time I hope that it might be recognized on grasss roots levels by people who see a glimpse of, and want, that something else.

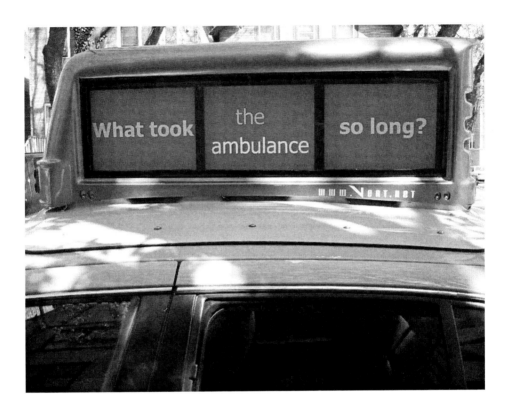

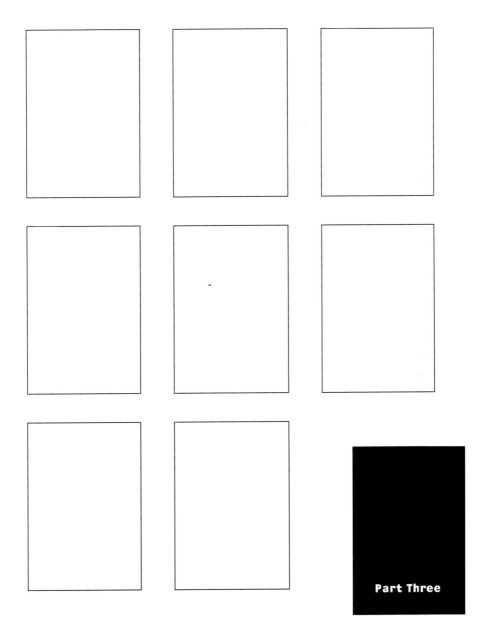

Part Three

Evaluations

Sarah Bennett, John Butler, Nicola Kirkham and Malcolm Miles

■ A Comparative Evaluation: Projects in Exeter, Barcelona, London, and Tyneside.

Introduction

This chapter compares ways in which the values of artists' interventions in urban social settings can be measured. This does not presuppose that any method of measurement is comprehensive but we hope by comparing four different cases that some of the problems of evaluation can be identified. The process of evaluation in the arts is relatively recent and there is no tried and tested methodology – those used range from the anecdotal to the audit-based – while some artists would argue that the value of their work is beyond audit. Against these arguments for intuitive appreciation, which follow the autonomy claimed for modern art, funding bodies are under pressure in our increasingly accounting culture to legitimise public investment in the arts, and arts organisations to improve their effectiveness. Between the two positions and overlooked from both, is a question as to who are the beneficiaries of art in social settings, and how they benefit. This is helpful in that it can offer specifics and redirects attention from art's production to its reception butb again, the answers are seldom easy to define. After all, if a work appeals to a non-specific public (such as commuters at a railway station), there is no way of knowing what revelation may occur, possibly long after the act in question, in the context of countless other factors. If complexity theory (derived from chaos theory) teaches us that small changes in conditions produce large changes in outcome for a given intervention, the challenge to the arts in saying what are the outcomes of such work is huge.

Nonetheless, a start can be made. We want to emphasise that the aim here is not to test and verify methods, nor to conclude that there is a correct way to evaluate arts projects. As we said above, it is to compare cases in order to identify problems for discussion and new questions for research. In making this start, we have selected four projects for which the aims are relatively clearly stated, in contrast to much of the public art investigated by Sara Selwood in *The Benefits of Public Art* (Selwood, 1995), for which the claims made were vague and undemonstrable. We have also selected these projects because they have been evaluated: the Window Sills project in Exeter was evaluated through feedback and dialogue carried out by a research assistant employed by the University of Plymouth; workshops with community groups in Sant Adrià de Besòs (adjacent to a major redevelopment zone in Barcelona) were documented and evaluated in terms of outcomes by the Polis Research Centre at the University of Barcelona; Visions of Utopia, a year-long programme of arts projects in the north of England, was evaluated in terms of public participation by the Arts Management Unit at the University of Northumbria at Newcastle – we look in particular at one project within it; and Killing Us Softly, a performance work by London-based artists' group

145

PLATFORM was evaluated through feedback sessions for participants and investigated through dialogue by another research assistant at the University of Plymouth. We hope the cases have enough in common to enable comparison – more bread and cheese than chalk and cheese – but are different enough in location, audience, content and form to raise different kinds of questions about their delivery of aims. The means of evaluation also differ and we enquire as to what extent it is possible to find appropriate means for specific kinds of projects, without mapping one model onto all. Each of the next four sections addresses one project in turn.

1. Window Sills

Window Sills was a research project initiated by staff from the School of Art and Design, University of Plymouth. The project was described and placed within a critical framework in Volume 1 of this series: *Locality, Regeneration and Divers[c]ities* (Bennett and Butler, 2000). This text does not repeat material given there but describes the evaluation processes used as an integral part of the project. It does, however, give some background for readers unfamiliar with the project. The evaluation processes used draw on both qualitative and quantitative methods and on material collected both during and after the project's timespan, including: interviews (15), questionnaires (73 completed), artists' reports (11), artists' diaries (2), comments books (2), visitor numbers and comments, anecdotal material, photographic documentation, peer review/case study (3), minutes of meetings (23) and observation. These formed the basis of an evaluation report that set the findings against the project aims and objectives. In that report we emphasise the value of qualitative evaluation over quantitative because the former can more fully elucidate the complexity of a project's outcomes as opposed to reducing experience to statistics. But we recognise, nonetheless, that methodologies for qualitative analysis continue to develop. We appreciate the limitations of any monitoring methods in telling a 'complete story'. This reflects the views of Francho Bianchini, who calls for 'new methodologies and indicators to measure the impact of cultural policies and activities in terms of quality of life, social cohesion and community development' (Bianchini cited by Shaw, 1999: 4). Additionally we have drawn material from an external evaluation undertaken by commissioned consultants: The Centre for Creative Communities (CCC).

Context

The project was led and managed by the University team: Sarah Bennett, John Butler and Research Assistant Gill Melling. It was the first project of this kind undertaken by the University's Fine Art area and advice was sought from artists experienced in this field of work other professionals working in related fields local organisations and funders. It was through the resulting reflection and strategy development that the shift from an initially prescriptive stance to an organic/responsive approach occurred which was profound in shaping our research. 'The Window Sills evaluation report indicates a high level of reflective practice...' (CCC, 2001:4).

As academics initially developing the project with research funding, we had both the privilege and the pressures of understanding where the project fitted into a broader picture of academic research within this field and challenging the status quo to develop new thought and praxis. We needed to establish the arts context for our project and our initial research revealed the difficulties of determining such a context. The project seemed to hover uncomfortably between the traditions of both community and public arts practices. The problem of locating our project was highlighted in the evaluation report on Window Sills by CCC. They state that 'Window Sills shares a great number of features with the community arts tradition, such as the emphasis on the centrality of the process, the collaborative nature of the project and the complex relationship between art and community work, particularly as it is reflected in the difficult role of the artist as catalyst and facilitator' (CCC, 2001:9). However, they also commented that 'If on the one hand, the initiators of Window Sills are keen to distance themselves from the prescriptive tradition of public art, it seems on the other, they still feel the need to be connected to that realm' (CCC, 2001:10).

The project was initially financially supported by internal University Research Funding, followed by a period making grant applications to external sources. The project successfully raised funding from the Arts Council South West (£1000), Regional Arts Lottery Programme (£29,500), Exeter Arts Council (£1,000), The Elmgrant Trust (£500) and the European League of Institutes of Arts (ELIA).

Concepts and Intentions

Window Sills aimed to examine the role of contemporary art practices in sustainable urban regeneration within non-metropolitan cities such as Exeter. Window Sills had two primary intentions in terms of 'inclusion': the inclusion of residents in cultural, critical and artistic activity to achieve new 'tools' to make decisions affecting their own lives and locality; and the inclusion of residents in the representation and expression of their own identities and locality.

> Window Sills is a process of critical and aesthetic enquiry on place, identity and civic participation (CCC 2001:1).

Implementation

Window Sills was a participatory art project which took place between June 1999 and July 2000. Commissioned artists Rebecca Eriksson, Edwina Fitzpatrick, Brendan Byrne and Neil Musson collaborated with residents from the West Exe district of Exeter on the related themes of personal identity and place/local history. The project actively engaged 259 participants in making collaborative artworks which were sited in and around the city. 'Great to see local residents and artists involved together to create slices of people's lives' (Visitor).

Networking was a fundamental strategy for Window Sills. We sought advice from local groups and their feedback enabled us to draw together a range of perspectives in order to understand the potential impact of the project. The interest, support and endorsement from organisations and individuals across the city made it feasible to develop the project and identify participants.

The project strategy was 'non-prescriptive' and 'open' to contributions by all participants. '… the collaborative and non-prescriptive nature of the project challenged the cultural dichotomy between artists and non-artists' (CCC, 2001:4). Some of the participating groups initially came up with ideas that were familiar (banners and murals) and suggested approaches and art forms that reflected their limited previous experiences. Through exchange about how ideas can be transformed into objects, both residents' and artists' awareness and knowledge of what was possible were extended.

> I have found that most people are very interested to discuss conceptual and ephemeral contemporary art. I felt on the whole that the project was successful in this aim because questions arose for participants such as: What is art? Why is this art? What is art for? And what does art do? (Artist).

As a result of the diversity of the participants involved in the project, a range of collaborative processes occurred enabling residents to engage in collaboration according to their own desires, abilities and personal circumstances. Some pre-existing groups opted to involve themselves in a collective manner. 'It has helped me to see that I have something to contribute' (Participant). Equally, facilitating people to tell their own stories and make their own interpretations of a theme through creative processes resulted in a diversity of identities being expressed. The way in which these processes were introduced by the artists depended on their own particular practice and the interests and abilities of the residents with whom they were collaborating.

> In this kind of project the needs and voice of the community become the steering force of the artistic direction, as the emphasis is on raising the visibility of marginalised communities… (CCC, 2001:4).

Evaluation

- The introduction of a collaborative, dynamic and fluid creative process is complex. For many participants the unfamiliarity of the creative process involved in making artwork(s) meant that preconceptions about the role of the artist needed to be addressed and the ability of the artists to communicate effectively helped to overcome these preconceptions. 'Working on the project has increased my skills and experience of liaising with publics, networking, co-ordinating, explaining, encouraging, facilitating, managing time tables and planning, workshop co-ordinating, both with participants and in the production/siting of the project' (Artist). We concluded that within this kind of practice the artist may find himself working as a facilitator or tackling the issue of shared authorship and needs to redefine his role to accommodate this. This required a shift in his sense of his own practice. 'For artists who have been trained to be the sole author and producer of artworks, collaborative approaches can only be possible through a process of self-reflection' (CCC, 2001:4). The most appropriate way we have found to describe the collaborative process and the interaction of artist and resident is that of exchange: it is a two-way process. 'The non-impositional and collaborative nature of the project questioned artists' ideas about what constitutes art practice' (CCC, 2001:3). A long-term and in-depth collaborative process can extend the critical understanding and skills of working with contemporary art practices for both artists and local participants. 'My role was as an artist and facilitator, not an art evangelist preacher. This was a difficult balance and an important question for me during the process' (Artist). We concluded that public art practices which impose objects on a public can be challenged by using an inclusive collaborative approach which engenders an ownership of the objects created and exhibited by local people.

- The involvement of artists in the early stages of the project as well as effective communication were needed to ensure that participants were not 'let down' at any stage. We had to allocate more of the artists' time in the early stages of the project than we had planned in order to build momentum and maintain contact with participants. The precise point at which the artists were included was a critical issue since early approaches to local organisations were crucial to establish the feasibility of the project. However, it was impracticable to employ the artists at the research and development stage, prior to funding being available. Owing to funding restraints, deadlines for research outputs and other external pressures, we had predetermined the time-scale for the completion of the project in the form of a 'final event'. Subsequently we realised that not only was it impossible to accommodate shorter or longer-term collaborations but also the exhibition of the artwork needed further consideration to find a format more appropriate to the organic and responsive strategies of the collaborations. We were surprised to discover that within a process-based project the end product remains an important focus for local people so that they can see evidence of their efforts. We concluded that in-built flexibility regarding the artist's roles, starting point and length of contribution and project completion, is essential for a responsive approach to collaborative and participatory arts initiatives.

> In leaving as many aspects of the making as possible to the collaborators (including materials and media to be used) and given the age and sometimes frailty of the participants, I was attempting to develop skills in materials and media as suggested by the collaborators and then dictated by the methodology, which needed far longer periods of experimentation.' (Artist).

- From the outset the project team realised the relevance of their research to government policy and current debates at local government level about inclusion. However, in retrospect, it also recognised that a greater amount of time for initial research would have more thoroughly underpinned the project and provided a broader context of work within this field. Although the consultative process proved invaluable, there nevertheless was a substantial amount of relevant material that subsequently came to light that would have further informed its research, planning and implementation. 'Any strategy for a collaborative arts initiative should include a sufficient period of time and funding for initial research' (Window Sills evaluation, 2002). Support from external professionals was essential in understanding, developing and supporting us in our project management strategies.

- The number of successful external funding applications was low in comparison with applications made and our evaluation concluded that this was due to the fact that our aims and objectives did not easily map onto the criteria used by funders. Our status as a University research project disadvantaged us because we were not perceived as sufficiently community based. More of an issue was the problem of trying to describe the outcomes of a temporary project to funders when the project was intended to be process led and 'open-ended', with no predetermined outcomes. CCC commented on this issue in its report

> Existing funding schemes may find it difficult to fund the great variety of locally generated projects as they often do not fit neatly into categories. Furthermore... most funding schemes still emphasise products as opposed to processes, thus process based initiatives can lack the economic resources to be successfully implemented and sustained (CCC, 2001:9).

CCC went on to comment that within broader funding contexts 'Participatory arts projects... have very little chance to compete for funds assigned to social or health services, particularly if they are temporary in nature' (CCC, 2001:9). As a result the project team was dependent on bidding internally for additional funding from the University, which was tied into the Research Assessment Exercise, and on gaining local 'in-kind' sponsorship and sharing resources through partnerships

- As an art practice in between traditional art forms (e.g. Public Art and Community Art), new parameters for judging inclusive collaborative art practice need to be used which must reflect project aims and objectives.

> Window Sills is in many ways a progressive project that successfully conducts a process of critical enquiry into the relationship between art and civic engagement. It is also proof that art today is increasingly defined by a theoretical framework that confers value and quality onto an object, as opposed to the intrinsic qualities of the process. Perhaps, in order to take the art truly out of the gallery, the organisers need to take the project out of the frame (CCC, 2001:10).

- In keeping with our aim to 'develop an inclusive and sustainable forum for creative thinking [and] decision-making', the involvement of participants in aspects of project decision-making, negotiation of objectives and strategies, was an effective method of empowerment, creating a sense of ownership. 'Really enjoyable...I liked the idea of involving local people in making art. It has brought Exeter local history alive. Well done and keep the project going!' (Participant). Local audiences were able to relate to an art practice that was driven by the 'voices' of local people thus increasing access to, and interpretation of, the work. Regional and national audiences are, however, difficult to attract to local projects. The project left a constructive legacy with the participants, their families and neighbours in terms of personal gains. The majority of the participants felt that the project was well managed and that they received a good level of support. However, a greater degree of follow up by the artists (subject to funding) after the final event would have ensured a clearer 'handing over' of their responsibilities to the participants or to other agencies. The project established an infrastructure for partnerships with local and city agencies and the success of this exchange has resulted in invitations to become involved in future projects, thus enhancing the possibility of sustainability.

> Participation in the arts can be an effective means for developing local capacity and for strengthening people's commitment to place. Thus, participatory art projects can act as catalyst for urban renewal, helping develop a sense of community, identity and self-esteem. Without planned follow-up, however, the effects can quickly dissipate. (CCC, 2001:7).

2. Sant Adrià De Besòs

Introduction:

A series of Civic Participation Workshops took place in Sant Adrià de Besòs between 1997 and 1999, during the period preliminary to the Universal Forum of Cultures to be held in Barcelona in 2004. They were devised by Dr Toni Remesar and Dr Enric Pol of the University of Barcelona, in part as a response to how the neighbourhood of Sant Adrià de Besòs, on the far side of the Besòs river from the municipality of Barcelona and near the Forum site, would be affected. While plans for the Forum were, and are, largely top-down, the participation workshops sought to introduce an alternative element of grass roots articulacy. The project was described in detail in *Advances in Art & Urban Futures Volume 1: Locality, Regeneration & Divers[c]ities*, prior to the evaluation process being completed. This paper seeks to include the general evaluation findings of the project.

Context

In 1995 the urban office of 'Barcelona Regional' applied for European Structural Funds for a regional project regenerating the river and creating an eight kilometre 'green belt' river park in Sant Adrià de Besòs.

Sant Adrià de Besòs is a small city, population 35,000, bordering Barcelona, which for a long time was a metropolitan 'dump' where marginalised communities had been rehoused and where polluting industries were located. The river Besòs, which divides the city into two large areas, acted as a territorial and social boundary. The proposed development had two elements. The eight kilometre park stretching inland and a 1.5 kilometre salt-water canal and marina where river met the sea. The project on paper appeared to be a good idea but was it the best solution? And were the social needs of the local population considered and attended to?

The local authority, wishing to link the two divided parts of the city, commissioned a newly-formed research group City Port Territory (CPT)[1] to look at how to use the river as a link. The group had been formed in 1996 in response to the Catalan government's desire to establish a quality structure for research into city development and regeneration. This interdisciplinary group was established by the University of Barcelona (UB), with membership comprising departmental representatives from Fine Arts, Economics, Environmental Psychology and Sociology (Chemistry was invited but declined to participate). From the outset the group had realised that Barcelona had an unusual waterfront stretching between two rivers, and it confirmed its interest in looking at an area where the two elements converged.

The group applied to the Spanish Ministry of Research for financial support for a research project, *Waterfronts and Urban Regeneration*, intended as a global survey under the auspices of the *Public Art Observatory* (PAO) – a network of European universities, co-ordinated by the UB, involved in interdisciplinary research on public art and urban regeneration. The application by City Port Territory was successful and it received a grant of 8,000.000 pesetas distributed over the period 1995 – 1999, with an extension of a further three years (1999 – 2002) and an additional budget of 1,750.000 pesetas.

It then met with the Office of Civic Participation at the City Council of Sant Adrià – a newly developed national scheme of regionally-based offices – to discuss the following major problems identified with this project – economic and environmental.

The *Public Art Observatory's* objective was to create a series of civic participation workshops critiquing the *Barcelona Regional*, looking at ways the river could be a central element of the city- a link rather than a barrier.

Intentions

The objectives of the workshops were:
- Participation – to empower the participation of the citizens in relation to thinking, planning and presenting public use proposals
- Information – to develop a system of civic information arrived from representation of the participants and where possible to disseminate the information amongst their civic groups (e.g. neighbourhood groups, cultural associations, etc.)
- Education – to educate participants in technical subjects and enable them to be capable of local and regional analysis. Through participation they can also learn how to consider the difference between desire/expectations and the logistics and viability of realisation
- Extension to the community – to enable a large proportion of the community to participate in the discussions and evaluate the outcomes.

Implememementation:

Civic Participation Workshops

For the participatory workshops to achieve their objectives the *Polis Research Centre* agreed it was necessary to involve as many of the constituency as possible. To facilitate this an inaugural meeting was organised, inviting representatives from all civic groups to discuss the ideas. A total of 120 citizens attended, representing 80–90 different groups. The first conclusion of the meeting was that it was impossible to work with such a large number of members and agreed that this should be reduced to 15–16 representatives. The civic groups then decided on the following representation: 5 x neighbourhood associations; 4 x NGOs (e.g. Red Cross) and 6 x other groups (e.g. sport, festival) and within one week the 15 representatives were selected.

The process started in an overly academic (scientific) way as a consequence of the Faculty of Economics representatives having little experience of managing participatory projects and at the suggestion of the Social Psychology Department,. At this point Toni Remesar, Director of *PAO*, was appointed as the link between the faculty and the local government.

The newly-formed group then began working with the 'Basin Authority' to gather technical information. Although the civic group representatives had no appropriate formal skills, following social science formal workshop methodologies they were able to analyse, in a non-directive way, the needs and problems facing the municipality of Sant Adrià de Besòs.

The workshops looked at the regeneration proposals for the river as central to the urban, social and community development of the city – the central topic being its social uses in the context of environmental regeneration. Two lists were generated - necessities and problems – which were analysed and later prioritised and proposals for solutions/resolutions offered by the workshops. A major conclusion *Polis* arrived at was that the two communities either side of the river faced away from each other, turning their backs on the river.

The *Polis Research Centre*, after completing the analysis, decided not to terminate the project and moved to:

Developing a pre - Master plan.

Introducing three PhD students, and using proven higher education teaching methodologies, Polis carried out an in-depth survey of the area – *walking the river and analysing the territory* – to get to know the place better. The outcomes sometimes contradicted findings that were claimed and made in the first phase of the project. The research students, through organising meetings and discussing proposals, looked for ways to realise the possibilities but they did not propose ideas – these belonged to the local citizens. The students used their professions and skills (architect, photographer/designer and draughtsman) to represent what the 'locals' wanted. This process lasted twelve months.

Following on from this process the objective to develop a pre-Master plan was agreed by all representatives. This was to be realised through a touring exhibition, funded by the city council, travelling to five venues, starting in the city centre – opened by the Mayor of the City and the Deputy Vice-Chancellor of Scientific Policy at the University of Barcelona – then moving around the neighbourhoods and concluding back in the centre with an accompanying symposium. The Director of *Barcelona Regional* , Mr. Acebillo, attended the symposium.

The exhibition, which took two months to prepare, proved to be the most difficult period of the project. This was largely due to *Polis* trying to find the best way to present the information in a basic structure of 'past, present and future' – that picked up the contents, phases, processes, aspects and essential proposals of the workshops.

As well as the more traditional static exhibition presentation, the group developed an accompanying CD-Rom, which presented Sant Adrià's statistical data, the fundamental aspects of *Barcelona Regional's* original project, statements on the project by representatives of all the political parties and evaluation of the project and resulting media impact. The two presentation elements allowed for a critical comparison between the civic and the technical proposals.

Although some local citizens did not agree with some of the proposals, by far the majority did agree with the general ideas.

Impact

As a consequence Platform Besòs 2004 was established – a civic and political platform for the regeneration of the area – and the fifteen civic group representatives who participated in the workshop were included in its membership. At a meeting of the civic forum in the city hall, the representatives presented a petition signed by 2,500 local residents (approx. 10% of adult population) supporting the 'master plan', against the official city plan.

Materially the official plan is still largely going ahead but the river as resource is central – bridging and linking both sides and a new transit line and a tramway is changing the transportation system.

Through questionnaires (verbal and written) the project concluded that the citizens of Sant Adrià de Besòs found identity through the process and weren't let down in their expectations. In fact the residents wished for the outcomes to be disseminated worldwide.

The participatory project has had a big impact in other national and international cities (e.g. Madrid – the Faculty of Fine Arts has worked with Mayor of Mosdoles, a 60s new town, in 'copying' the project; a city in Argentina is also scrutinising the project; and the project has been the model for the development of the participatory actions of the Portuguese Centre of Design in the district of Marvila in Lisbon).

Skills gained by the participants included: visualising (e.g. photographic), communication, team working, employment in local authority in the environmental department and political argument (mobilised community). Others such as research skills were not transferred because of the shortage of time created by the demand of the city for results.

Politically the project had a considerable impact on the political parties: left wing political parties have changed the way they communicate and mobilise the community; the Socialist Party adopted strategies for developing policies using formal participatory processes; the Communist Party used more participatory/action.

The selection of the appropriate PhD research students was also very important and the point at which they were introduced proved critical. Key aspects of their roles were:
- facilitation rather than mediation
- the process of managing communication
- exploring the relationship between economic drivers and social factors (quality of life).

Evaluation

- This kind of participatory project needs sufficient time – a minimum of two years

- The process is more important than products

- It is important, but difficult to work with environmentalists – problems of regulations and audit

- Scientists/chemists especially from universities are reluctant to be involved in these forms of projects – a political decision, through a fear of repercussions of a negative report

- It was important to include research students working in an interdisciplinary way in Social Sciences and Architecture. This indicated a shift from the tradition of only involving Fine Art trained researchers and may be a result of the changing roles of the artist, moving to non-artefact based practice

- The research students need to be introduced during the second phase of the project

- The emphasis of this type of project needs to be focused on social (environmental) regeneration rather than economic imperatives

- As a consequence the focus for the regeneration is on ideas for a 'natural' centre, with less focus on the more structural aspects of the project – *auto organising* process

- The impact on the population can be considerable, not only if the authorities adopt all or even part of any civic proposals for urban regeneration, but also if they incorporate the processes into in their political and management strategies. Generally, however, local authorities are not interested in the process used in these projects.

- Communication is vitally important and the use of language to explain ideas to different audiences is critical in empowering the participants. During the project the groups found that it was necessary to have an interlocutor to link them.

- Other methodologies must be explored – the *Polis* developed the methodology of the *CPBoxes* (Comments and Patterns Boxes) that has been implemented in the neighbourhood of the Poblenou in Barcelona, and in the district of La Mina in Sant Adrià de Besòs.[2]

3. Visions of Utopia

Context

The *Visions of Utopia* Festival was coordinated in 1997 by Esther Salamon, Co-Director of Artists Agency in Sunderland (since renamed Helix Arts and relocated to Newcastle). It operated across the north of England as umbrella for forty-eight local projects and events. Planning for the project began in 1994 with consultation of organisations, community groups and individuals in the region, which includes major conurbations as well as agricultural and industrial villages, using contacts from the agency's previous work. Artists Agency had a track record in building up such contacts in local and health authorities and with community-based arts groups. Several of the individual projects were also integral to local arts development. One, The Seen and the Unseen, was a multi-project programme for art–science collaborations on ecological issues such as water pollution. Typical of work pioneered by Artists Agency was an artist's residency in the Northumbria Police and Probation Authority – *Future Lives Indifferent Spaces* – based in the probation service at South Shields. Each project found its own funding. Artists Agency offered co-ordination, advice, support and production of a colour brochure. Central funding was difficult to raise, Salamon thinks because the Festival 'was a wacky concept, not attractive to corporates and difficult to categorise'. The latter is confirmed by a survey respondent in the evaluation: 'the project ... tried to be too many things for too many people, so it has given a confused message. It is not easy to explain to anyone and so has missed out on the level of profile it could have achieved' (Farley and Cashman, 1999: 14). The probation service project, which ran into the following year, produced a digitally imaged calender for 1999. It was evaluated by Rebecca Farley and Stephen Cashman of the University of Northumbria at Newcastle, whose Arts Management Unit had carried out such evaluations for some years for regional arts organisations. The same researchers carried out a broader evaluation of Visions of Utopia as a whole. We refer to both below.

Concept and Intentions

The aim of *Visions of Utopia* – subtitled Art, Science and Thought for a New Millennium – was to see if a small arts organisation could be a catalyst to radical thinking about society and could actively involve local people in talking about their ideas of a better world; and to enable people in the north of England to 'think the impossible' and 'wonder what would happen if ...'. Its letterhead states: 'the aim is to enable everyone to identify and explore visions of better lives and the better worlds they would like to inhabit'. Opening up ways of thinking about the shaping of society was more important to Salamon than success in terms of arts funding or the attention of the art world and its press and being independent of aesthetic judgements. The Festival was in part a way to celebrate the diversity of arts provision in the northern region and to link local and potentially overlooked projects in a larger programme more likely to generate publicity and public participation. Elements of the Festival took place in Cumbria, Northumbria, County Durham, Teesside and Tyne and Wear. Half were in Newcastle, attracting audiences of around 10,000 in all (Farley and Cashman, 1999: 2, 6). The scale of participation envisaged ranged from audiences of 20 or so for local projects to 3,000 for the biggest events.

Implementation

The Festival opened with a lantern parade at sunset on 20th September in Ulverston, the fifteenth such organised annually by Welfare State International. Four processions converged bearing home-produced lanterns a foot high to hang on a beacon. This was later dismantled and taken to South Shields for a parade at sunrise on 7th November, symbolically linking the west and east of the northern region. The Festival brochure states: 'The tower can only be made with contributions from each neighbourhood and as a community beacon it is an ideal symbol of Utopia. An assemblage of light. A delicate gift representing the whole community'. The link to Welfare State International ensured that this opening event was likely to succeed. Salamon sees the lantern procession as becoming grounded in a local environment, its continuation and scale evidence of local support. For Welfare State International it is a re-invention of traditions displaced by industrialisation. The *Evening Mail* (22 September 1997) ran a two-page feature:

> As I approached Ulverston's Ford Park I caught the echo of a distant drum beat. The whiff of smoke was in the air and I caught sight of the flaming torches lighting up the park. Ghostly white shapes cluttered up the playing field and streets, swaying in the breeze ... Local People had created paper lanterns on the theme 'Visions of Utopia' and the result was magical. People had let their imagination run riot. There were cats, trees, robots, and a lighthouse with wings. ... the beer-drinkers and would-be clubbers that usually line the streets were replaced by families, their eyes shining under the glow of 300 or so paper lanterns ... (Zoe Green)

Quoting the text at length brings out certain qualities: on one hand, the emotive image of smoke and torches; on the other, a celebration of imagination, and a note of conviviality, or nostalgia, as families take the place of lager-drinkers.

The lantern procession, en route from Cumbria to Tyneside, was repeated at Wansbeck, Northumberland. The *News Post Leader*, under the heading 'Lake spectacular launches festival' and leading its story with the annual Wansbeck Festival's adoption of the utopian theme, states: 'The spectacular event at the end of the parade will reflect utopian dreams and the closing of summer into autumn' (*News Post Leader*, 1 October, 1997). An imaginary island was constructed in the lake at Queen Elizabeth II Park 'to house the dreams and realities of the people of Wansbeck' as the brochure put it.

This, an annual event aligned to *Visions of Utopia*, was one of the largest, involving MidNAG community choir, six local schools, dancer Tim Rubidge, Dodgy Clutch Theatre Company and Trinity Youth Group. The closing procession across the causeway to St. Mary's lighthouse at Whitley Bay took place on 28th November 1997 in foul weather. Barrels of burning tar lit up the causeway as light projections moved across the surface of the tower. Standing on the spiral staircase within, a choir sang for the North Sea.

The Festival included events in which participants looked to their future environments and social situations. Asked, 'What will our society look like in 100 years time?' one school group responded: 'modern ... full of cars ... too many cars ... full of car parks ... shops and car parks ... we'll have solar power ... there won't be any here, there's hardly any sun ... pedal power ... it'll take hours to get anywhere ... polluted ... there'll be loads of rubbish ... worse than it is now ... this school will still be painted pink ... it's scabby ... needs to be redecorated'. Another group described an ideal world as 'peaceful, fun, respectful, education, health, cleaner, no litter' (unattributed voices, May 1997, transcripts supplied by Artists Agency). Children aged 6–16 in South Moor, Stanley, Co. Durham, produced a model of the county as they foresaw its appearance in 2100. Education worker Steve Grey commented: 'We know that South Moor is far from Utopia at the moment, but the kids have come up with a lot of ideas of how housing and the transport infrastructure will change the look of the place' (*The Northern Echo*, 30 August 1997). Amongst reflections of current environmental debate in the model were wind and solar power, a monorail and a moving pavement.

The collaboration with the Northumbria Probation Service, with whom a link was established in 1989, grew out of *Visions of Utopia* and continued after the closing performance. It entails six artists' residencies, one in each of the areas covered by the service, beginning in 1998. They offer participation to a client-group perceived by the public and the state as socially excluded and felt by Artists Agency to be likely to benefit from the communicative aspects of an art project and from the acquisition of skills seeded by a professional artist.

Digital artist Sharron Lea-Owens worked with the South Shields Community Supervision Team in a programme for the rehabilitation of young offenders, with technical support from Sunderland University's Department of Photography. Using digital imaging, participants produced a calendar, each month represented by a different person's work. Lea-Owens saw her role as facilitator: 'I initiated the project on the understanding that the images produced would be the clients' images' (Farley, 1999: 5), and officers of the Supervision Team saw the project as offering structured activities, skill acquisition and a way to fill time. One officer responded that people become offenders when they have nothing else to do, so that developing skills and finding links to a project or group in which they can fulfil their potential will also help reduce rates of offending (see Farley, 1999: 6).

Evaluation

Visions of Utopia included many events involving public participation in art-making. 19,055 people attended events, another 10,092 participated actively as co-producers, and there were 5,683 visitors to the Festival website (Farley and Cashman, 1999: 6, 10). About thirty schools and youth groups in the region took part in a project with the Northumbria Police Authority area, making a 1000-sq.ft jigsaw of utopian imagery. Danny Gilchrist, coordinator of Northumbria Coalition Against Crime, said: 'We hope this project will have a lasting impression on the children and help them reflect on what sort of world they want to grow up in' (The Journal, 23 October 1997).

A contrast appears. The University of Northumbria report is strong on audit, measuring numbers of participants while including survey responses and findings from consultation with arts groups. It gives a breakdown of such figures by county and art form: 48.9% in Tyne and Wear, 8.5% in Northumberland, 19.1% in Durham, 14.9% in Cumbria, 6.2% in Teesside, and 2.1% in touring events; 6.7% literature, 16.7% drama, 33.3% art, 3,3% digital media, 6.7% music, 3.3% film, 16.7% mixed media, and 6.7% non-art projects. But the reports in local newspapers give anecdotal, chatty (one might say journalistic) stories which nonetheless convey the feeling of the event in question, at least for the reporter and probably not just for the him or her. Some of the figures are more interesting than others – for example that 13.3% of events were intended for audiences of fewer than twenty people, an imaginative investment in intimate cultural exchange; a further 26.7% were for audiences from 20 to 100, and a further 26.7% for those between 100 and 500. The report also lists sixteen separate aims found in the collated statements of a sample of thirty projects, adding that ten of these project teams or organisations saw them as having been very successful and fourteen successful. The report's conclusion praises Visions of Utopia for reaching a wide audience, being a broad umbrella which supported diversity and satisfying 80% of survey respondents.

The evaluation of the Probation Service project differs from that of the Festival as a whole in placing more emphasis on participant response (from young offenders, necessarily anonymous in its findings, and officers). It is thus more anecdotal but (for us) closer to actuality. It separates out the expectations of the artist, Sunderland University, the clients (on probation) and staff. Lea-Owens, for instance, says:

> I didn't want it to be like an environmentalist, hippy, liberal calendar. I was also aware [of] this undercurrent (mainly from probation officers) that the only people interested in this project would be people with mental health difficulties or drug issues ... they're the only lot allowed to have visions (cited in Farley, 1999: 7).

She saw the quality of images made by participants as high and a calendar which could be on every probation officer's desk as more effective than an event, though there was an exhibition at the end of the project. She also sees a shift in the direction of her own work:

> ... the subject of my work has altered as a result of the project. I used to create images that explored the fetters of a gendered and ethnic identity, but the interaction with one offender taught me that the tag of being labelled criminal was a far more sinister and prevailing imposition ... I began to produce CCTV performances in public spaces (cited in Farley, 1999: 10).

On the residency in general, the report says: 'There seem to have been few major problems or crises within the project and the problems that were encountered were overcome or managed in some way' (Farley, 1999: 8). For the participants, the evaluation report states a positive experience entailing new skills and a greater feeling of self-worth – the latter affirmed by several personal statements.

> Not as many clients were involved as had been hoped, yet the project was a very positive experience for the clients in a core group ...The favourable way the calender and exhibition were received by probation officers, friends and relatives gave a real boost to clients' self-esteem (Farley, 1999: 14).

Everyone interviewed gave a positive view, which makes the project appear a genuine contribution to improving the experience of being on probation in the region and possibly (but this is not audited and would be a long-term process) to reducing crime if that follows higher self-esteem among potential offenders. On the question of self-esteem, however, this report highlights a quality frequently central to arts projects in health and welfare settings, where some or most of the participants have been categorised in various ways as marginal people and where raising self-esteem may be the first step to a recovery (or development) of social skills and citizenship.

Finally, *Visions of Utopia* produced 30,000 brochures circulated throughout the region. These included a programme of events and a reply-paid card on which respondents could give their personal vision of utopia. Only around thirty such visions were received (0.1%), which would suggest a poor result in quantitative terms. However, the point may be to ascertain qualitatively the imagination and hope entailed in those responses which were received. For instance, one which (to paraphrase) proposes a world of sharing and friendliness, in which noone suffers injustice, where citizens are co-workers and the social ethos non-violent. It makes no sense to audit visions, yet without them there would be no social progress, only reproduction.

4. Killing Us Softly

The project Killing Us Softly has been developed by Dan Gretton of the artists' group Platformas a means to greater understanding of the mind-set which allows otherwise rational people to carry out acts which have consequences which are fatal or otherwise disastrous for those affected. It takes the form of small-scale performances, for an audience of eight sitting in black-painted cubicles observing a narrator and visual aids. Initially consisting of a four-hour performance-lecture witnessed in silence and followed by discussion, the event has since extended to a ten-hour programme including a facilitated discussion. The material spans the administration and planning of the Holocaust, the persecution of minorities in the Balkans in the 1990s and the management and impacts of the transnational oil industry.

Context

Killing Us Softly is contextualised by a larger thematic project entitled 90° *Crude*, which began in 1996. It forms one specific exploratory thread of 90° *Crude's* investigation of the ethical questions affected by corporate business networks. The historical context of both projects is *Homeland*, which began in 1993 to problematise the incorporeal nature of the relationships of different cultural contexts within networks of energy production and consumption. The *Homeland* project deconstructed the UK's electricity supply, from its sites of production in Wales, Portugal and Hungary, through to the corporate headquaters of the central administrator of this process in London. This UK touring exhibition (as part of London International Festival of Theatre) accumulated over 300 recorded interviews in which people discuss their dis-connection from the production sources of electricity they consume in their everyday lives. Thus the distanced responsibility of consumers and in particular of the corporations as principally London-based producers was the unresolved issue which became the field of exploration of *Killing Us Softly* within the general thematic concern to investigate still further and in various ways, corporate business networks of energy production, for which oil became the focus for 90° *Crude*.

This context is important because it charts the interdependent development of each project to the Platforms group's overall intentions, methodologies and the thematic scope of the practice in general over the last ten years. It is important to note, then, although *Killing Us Softly* can be considered the work of a sole artist, and as an entirely autonomous lecture-performance piece, it is also a part of the wider creative exploration of Platform's concern for human rights, ecology, environment, culture and social change as material for art. *Killing Us Softly* tested new material and a specific strategy of communicating these complex ideas amongst an initial community of interest.

Concept and Intentions

The idea for *Killing Us Softly* was developed as a hypothesis by Dan Gretton to explore ethical implications of the effects of disconnected responsibility within corporate-led capitalism. Dan Gretton's hypothesis asserted a proximity of corporate psychology and bureaucracy today with historical examples of genocide. From his research into historical studies of perpetrator psychology in Nazi Germany, Dan Gretton explored the notion, which first came to prominence during the Eichmann trials in 1961, of the Schreibtischtäeter or desk-murderer; a person who however distanced from the actuality of murderous acts, fuels them nevertheless. Research shows morality is sustained between the individual and the system in such cases by an extreme form of rationality, that of the compartmentalisation of different facets of reality. Thus *Killing Us Softly* allied psychological compartmentalisation and its relation to the bureaucratic structures of corporations (with its obvious relation to the fordist production-line) with the wider cultural context of global corporate capitalist culture, as a system in which we are all ethically implicated.

The intention of *Killing Us Softly* was to exemplify the contemporary ethical relevance of the research findings. This implied the communication of the proximity of contemporary corporate mentality and ways of thinking to the historic, purportedly distant occurrence of the Jewish Holocaust as a matter of profound social significance. Moreover, to provide in support of this hypothesis, historic evidence of corporate collusion in genocide (for instance the role of existing oil corporations in fueling the Nazi regime). However, it was thought the presentation of the research, rather than simply encourage a rationalised engagement with the material (for example as pedagogy by presenting in lecture form to a lay audience), should also allow an experiential understanding to emerge. Neither, it was thought, should a performative distance between the content of the material and its mode of delivery misconstrue its essential intentions as 'theatre'. The necessarily experimental nature of this project (being neither lecture nor performance but perhaps a bit of both) has meant that no two performances, in content or form, have yet been the same; the project must continuously develop, ultimately to ensure its artistic presentation sustains the shocking contemporary resonance of the material.

Implementation

'The process begins with a phone call' (Dan Gretton interview with the artist 2002)

To test the material and the formal strategies of its presentation Phase One of *Killing Us Softly* consisted of five lecture-performances (or voyages) given at seven week intervals from December 1999 to June 2000. A total of forty specially selected individuals were invited to attend in intimate groups of eight to nine. Each event was a five to seven hour long lecture-performance given in Platform's London residence, followed immediately by an audience discussion space over dinner on a Thames boat ride. The audience members were already known to Dan Gretton through previous Platform events or they were contacted via Platform's extended network for their potential professional interest in the subject matter. Each event was organised so that the members of each group had never previously met. The audience included interdisciplinary groups of activists, academics, corporate employees and artists. The attendance of a professional psychologist was deemed essential for each event to test the central tenet of the research – psychological compartmentalisation. The audience commitment in general was also essential and was emphasised in the initial phone conversations and in a follow-up letter (for each of the nine people committed to attend the events, an average of thirty people were contacted by telephone). A further letter sent one month prior to the actual event warned commited audience members about the shocking nature of the work and asked for a final confirmation of their commitment. This letter also gave written instructions about the length (but not the specific content or nature) of the event, what clothing to prepare and also noted they should arrive fifteen minutes prior to the event, to remain silent upon entering the building, to refrain from taking notes in any form and to hand their watches to the usher upon arrival. The intensity and disciplinary nature of the environment was created so as to discombobulate, isolate, comfort and consciously instruct the experience of the viewing audience, that is to set the event as an individualised experience, apart from everyday reality and thus to exemplify the intentions of the project.

The Program of *Killing Us Softly*
Concept: Dan Gretton
Lecture-Performance: Dan Gretton
Music: Jane Trowel
Set: Nick Edwards, James Merriot
Boat facilitation: James Merriot, Emma Sangster, Jane Trowell
Development/Support: James Merriot, Emma Sangster, Ute Spittler, Jane Trowel

1st Voyage
Saturday 11th December 1999, 13:00 – 19:30
Participants: Peter Butcher, David Butler, Nick Edwards, Mark Ellis, Claire Gordon,
        Wallace Heim, Greg Muttit, Emma Sangster, Ute Spittler
From Fields: Youth employment, economics, philosophy, anti-corporate activism,
        psychology, contemporary visual arts, ecological design

2nd Voyage
Saturday 29th January 2000, 13:00 – 20:00
Participants: Zibby Campbell, Patrick Field, Ann Kinsman, Denis Marechal,
        MalcolmMiles, Steve Parry, Helena Paul, Anna Wright
From Fields: Theatre, education, cultural criticism, community activism, ecology,
        human rights, psychology.

3rd Voyage
Saturday 18th March 2000, 13:30 – 20:45
Participants: Mark Brown, Rabhya Dewshi, Gareth Evans, Miche Fabre Lewin,
        Corrine Gretton, Rodney Mace, Derek Wax.
From Fields: Psychology, cultural criticism, contemporary visual arts,
        anti-corporate activism, counselling, history, documentary television,
        Jewish Studies

4th Voyage
Saturday 6th May 2000, 13:30 – 20:45
Participants: Nicky Childs, Charlotte Leonard, Emma McFarland, Tim Nunn,
        Heike Roms, Andy Rowell, Ben Salt, Nick Stewart
From Fields: Live arts, corporate finance, photography, theatre criticism,
        ecological activism, education.

5th Voyage
Saturday 24th June 2000, 13:30 – 20:45
Participants: Colin Clark, Alsion Craig, Carla Drahorad, Bob Fraser, Rosey Hurst,
        John Jordan, Sue Palmer, Kate Wilson.
From Fields: Internet radio, psychology, finance journalism, archivism, corporate
        ethical consultancy, direct action, ecological campaigning, performance art.

The lecture-performance given by Dan Gretton was supported by the staged physical environment, the visual imagery (slides and video clips) and live music or 'soundtrack' performed by a violist. Dan Gretton was intimately placed at the centre of a darkened space in a face-to-face interaction with members of the audience, each isolated in cubicles from the other. Each cubicle contained a chair with space enough for one person to sit. Each audience member was also given a blanket and a glass of water by the artist at the start of the performance. During the fifteen minute interval (this developed to two by voyage five) audience members were shown to a adjoining room for refreshments. The space for discussion after the event was provided by dinner on a Thames boat ride through the City of London district. Audience members were ushered by a member of Platform from the space of the performance (the Platform office) to the boat moored on a nearby jetty. It was made clear to the audience that conversations on the boat were to be recorded and a transcript made by the artist for the purposes of developing each of the project's future voyages.

Evaluation

Evaluation has been and continues to be an essential aspect of *Killing Us Softly*. Following the initial two year preparation of the project's hypothesis and prior to its 'public' lauch in Phase One, a pilot performance of the research material was given by Dan Gretton to Jane Trowell and James Merriot – co-members of Platform. Following this event, held at the artist's home, their appraisal led to the official test lecture-performance with an initial wider community of interest in Phase One as noted above. The highly evolved and detailed process of feedback from participants incorporated into the performance-lecture events has extended both the concept of *Killing Us Softly* and its audience. It is also interesting to note that audience members are in fact referred to by Dan Gretton as participants. All feedback from participants throughout the project has been recorded, debated and archived.

The process of evaluation includes:
* Facilitated discussion on the day during a boat-trip
* A written or verbal feedback form
* Group feedback days

Outcomes – Phase two

The intensely considered lecture-performances of *Killing Us softly* to an average audience of eight people and the subsequent strength of responses and openness to engage further in the project development of its forty participants has had perhaps the most profound effect on Platform (as a group in general) which has developed a sense of the absolute integrity of the interaction between its work and its audience. In essence the outcome has been a profound sense of commitment extending to all projects within *90% Crude*. Platform is currently re-conceptualising the notion of 'production' to fit the nature of the success of its projects, away from the traditional performance model (of production following research and development) towards a much more fluid and dynamic model that can evolve and respond in a variety of forms (alternative media, publications, film, etc). This leads Platform away from traditional models of efficient practice towards a process that will continue to personally invite people, write to them, and create a feedback process of questionaires and feedback days. In conventional performance terms this seems an inefficient method but it responds to the intensity and strength of the continued participation in Killing Us softly which exceeds traditional notions of audience interest.

Killing Us Softly (Phase Two) now incorporates further research and development to extend its presentation to new audiences using new media with new and revised material. The central concern of this phase was to 'target two groups of professionals who are central to the development of Killing Us Softly – psychologists and corporate employees – with the aim of attracting one individual from both fields to collaborate with Platform on a medium/long-term basis' (Dan Gretton, Report to London Arts).

On-going Research

The conceptual development of the project was effected by two research trips taken during Phase Two. The first was a visit to the Saurer Factory in Arbon in August 2000. Saurer, now a textile factory, manufactured specially designed lorries during World War II that were used to gas 400,000 Jews from Chelmo in Poland and an investigation into how such a corporation becomes genocidal plays a central role in Killing Us softly. The trip allowed new information to be gathered, including photographic documentation of the now derelict factory buildings and interviews with individual employee's including Saurer's head of corporate communications, Dr. Carole Ackerman. The issue of 'corporate amnesia' was exemplified in a statement by Dr. Ackerman. 'We don't live on history…we don't live on the past' will feature in further performances of Killing Us Softly and an article about the trip by Platform exploring this issue in more detail. In December 2000 a trip to Zimbabwe had a profound effect on Dan Gretton's understanding and appreciation of 'the continuum of the colonial mind-set' (Dan Gretton, statement in Platform letter to London Arts). The British colonial legacy in Zimbabwe, more specifically the legacy of Cecil Rhodes and his corporations such as the British South Africa Company and De Beers, were the focus of the substantial research and visual documentation which were gathered. The most powerful experiences, however, were personal – a ritual act of atonement for colonialisation on the grave of Rhodes in the Matobo hills, witnessing a ceremony to mark the handover of a friend's father's fishing business to the Zimbabwe government and listening to a tobacco farmer rage against 'squattors' occupying 'his' land. Several of these experiences were woven into the two performances of Killing Us Softly in Phase Two. The structure of the first of these events is noted below:

- Introduction – Parallel Time Experiences (VE Day/Helmsbrechts death march/ Bosnia camp)
- Dan Grettons Journey. The Holocaust and Transnational corporations (Ken Sarowiwa and Nigeria)

- Establishment of central thesis – parallel white collar aspects of Nazism & transnational corporations today (Albert Speir and John Brown)

(15 minute Break)

- Historiography of the Holocaust
- Questions of cultural proximity (Britain and Germany)
- Saurer Lorry corporation'[s memorandum
- Invisibility of corporations (Shell and BP fueling Nazi Germany; I.G .Farben, Hennes)
- Dan Gretton's journey to Arbon (Saurer Headquarters)
- Oil Executive in his London garden (Port Harcourt oil trails)

(15 minute Break)

- Development of genocidal psychology in Europe (Germany in SW Africa)
- Brtish Empire – The continuum from Empire to transnational corporations (slavery and banking)
- Dan Gretton's journey to SW Africa – Zimbabwe

(15 minute Break)

- Desk murderer – The doctors of the Wannsee conference
- 'Hard' and 'soft' killing – differential judgements (Walter Stier, a Nazi transport official – 'I never left my desk')
- Dan Gretton, journey from Weimar to Buchenweld
- Today's corporations in Nazi Germany
- Dan Gretton's Grandmother's corporate shares – What is our comfort built upon?
- A methodology of perpetrator psychology? – 6 common strands (incrementalism, normalization, linguistic de-humanization, an avoidance of physical violence, distancing, compartmentalization)
- Imagination of a different world (Marcus and Berger)

Between January and April 2001 Dan Gretton and an additional research assistant Emma Sangster (employed specifically for *Killing Us Softly* one day a week) conducted extensive UK wide research in the fields of social psychology, social anthropology and sociology to determine whether any academic research had been completed into the compartmentalisation of the mind/desk-murderer question relating to individuals working in corporations: No research was found.

On-going dialogues and relationships with psychologists and corporate employees: have been successfully established in the second phase of the project. The following people were amoung those who attended the last three performances of *Killing us Softly*:

Patrick Neyte – Head of Environment, Health & Safety, Code of Conduct Department for Levi's (Europe, Middle East and Africa)

Charlotte Leonard – Finance Director, Virgin Energy

Sara Boas – Director of Boas Consulting, Brussels (extensive experience of working with oil industry executives)

Dr. Martin Hartmann, author of several books on Management Consultancy

Bob Fraser – Director of Bloomberg Business News

Rosey Hurst – Director of Impactt (an environmental consultancy firm)

David Hockin – Design Director of C.I.M.E.X.

Jock Encombe – Corporate psychologist and partner in Young Samuel Chambers Ltd.

A repeated response of these participants was the need for others in their sectors to experience the work and for participants to continue their own engagment with the project. Pat Neyts expressed his desire for several colleagues at director level within Levi's to come to the next event, while Sara Boas made the following statement

> *Your work is, in my view, quite stunning and outstanding. It had a significant impact on me and I would like to continue to be engaged with what you are doing*

Such responses from the second phase of the project have proved corporate employees can and will engage with the extremely provocative nature of Killing Us Softly. It has, however, become apparent to Platform that finding a 'corporate insider' is going to be a complex and long process demanding a more sensitive approach than the current strategy of extending the audience of the project through public advertising. Shiela O'Donnell, a private investigator based in California, works with corporate whistle-blowers and is now guiding and helping with the preparation of this aspect of the project. This currently includes developing the necessary provisions of a guaranteed anonymity or 'safe space' for the individuals concerned.

In a meeting with Professor Tony Ryle, the world's leading authority on Cognitive Analytic Therapy, the central tenet of the hypothesis of Killing Us Softly was in research terms confirmed as unprecedented, timely and of great interest. It was suggested by Prof. Ryle that should Platform wish to collaborate on an academic basis, the corporate interviewing aspect would make an extremely good research project for a psychology student. This collaboration is currently in discussion.

Three further lecture-performance events werestaged on 24 June 2000, 9 June and 23 June 2001; this second cycle integrated substantial new sections, especially emphasising the narrative aspect of the work relating to the personal journeys of Dan Gretton to the Saurer factory in Arbon and the Zimbabwe journey/legacy of British Empire research. This, it is felt, has strengthened the work, providing a richer narrative strand to complement the more theoretical aspects of the research. Other presentations of extracts from Killing Us Softly have been given at 'Between Nature', a conference held at Lancaster University, and a public lecture at Headlands Centre for Arts, San Francisco on 19 August 2001.

An extremely strong 'community of interest' has been established among those who have participated in the events in both Phase One and Phase Two. Many individuals have been overwhelemd by the power of the event and the ideas behind it. This has been reflected in the feedback process (as detailed in the Evaluation section) from which Platform have documented several hundred pages of written and verbal responses to the work from participants. Two further, specially organised feedback days had the dual benefit of creating an extremely strong sense of ongoing commitment to the work from those who have experienced it while also providing invaluable assistance to the Plaform team in its development of 90° *Crude*.

A feedback day was held at *Platform* on 9 July 2000 attended by sixteen participants in Phase One of *Killing Us Softly*. The day was a response to the participants' enthusiasm for such an event expressed in the feedback forms and for a desire to develop and support the work further, particularly to provide emotional back-up for participants wanting to explore the work, to share information on the project's key themes and to question the nature of engagement of the audience in the project. A second feedback day held on 24 July 2000 following the requested agenda set by the first meeting focused on the role of the psychologist in the project's future development. The feedback days generated two practical support groups:

- Production Sub-Group consisting of Nick Childs (Artsadmin), Heike Roms (University of Aberystwyth), Nick Stewart (video artist) and Tim Nunn (photographer 7 producer), who met together with the project co-ordinators Dan Gretton and Emma Sangster, for the first time on 18 May 2001. Much of this meeting revolved around the issue of how to disseminate this work to a wider audience without losing the intensity and intimacy of the events held in Phase One at the Platform space. Others venues such as the London Roundhouse Crypt were explored but the sub-group came down strongly in favour of keeping events in the Platform space and continuing to limit the audience size to a maximum of nione people. However, members of the sub-group strongly recommended developing a vigorous culture around these events, that is by using film/video, publications and internet link-ups to the performances so that the central ideas can extend to a much wider audience.

- Conceptual sub-group consisting of twelve participants from Phase One and who have subsequently met in April 2001, May 2001 and January 2002 to explore certain of the themes in the project. This has included a screening of Claude Lanzmann's film *Shoah* which was held at the Weinar Library in central London, followed by a discussion.

Documentation of *Killing Us Softly* was made consisting of a complete audio recording (by Sue Palmer, participant and radio producer), a video recording (by Nick Stewart, participant and video artist) and photographic stills of the lecture-performance (by Emma Sangster). A research archive consisting of forty thematic sections includes articles, press clippings, images, leaflets and related documentation used by *Killing Us Softly*. An eight page introductory document produced in March 2001 by Dan Gretton and Emma Sangster as a means to address some of the key themes of the project was distributed to a select number of participants for their comments. John Berger responded,

> *Killing us Softly is very strong. You're right, I'm sure, about the urgent, urgent need for new structures of narrative and formulation... Thank-you for the offerings. They mean so much to me*

Conclusion

Among the many questions which arise from these four cases of projects which have undergone some form of evaluation are:

- whether qualitative or quantitative methods offer more appropriate understandings of a project's delivery
- whether there are advantages in employing external evaluators
- whether anecdotal information is helpful
- whether, indeed, to attempt to measure reception is useful.

To take these in order: three of the projects (*Window Sills*, the workshops in St Adrià de Besòs, and *Killing Us Softly*) rely mainly on qualitative evaluation. This is carried out through (variously) observation, interviews and informal discussion, and by estimating the impact of a project through actions and policy decisions which follow it. An advantage of such an approach is that it allows evaluators to gain a rounded impression of a project, by meeting participants (both professional and non-professional) face to face. It also gives an opportunity to question the key instigators, and follow up their responses with further, perhaps unpredicted, questions. This may be thought to produce a more multi-faceted picture than that given by statistics alone. Having said which, *Window Sills* did include data (such as the number of successful funding bids) in its evaluation. Equally, the research team in St Adrià de Besòs built up a copious volume of documentation and probably gained influence with planning authorities in proportion to the extent of participation in their workshops. In contrast, *Killing Us Softly* is more self-contained, evolving through continuing use of feedback from previous participants as well as the developmental processes undergone by the artists themselves.

Visions of Utopia was evaluated by a unit considerably experienced in such matters, revealing the extent and geographical distribution of participation by individuals. This information is useful to funding bodies and arts organisations with a regional remit in identifying how far the arts reach to places outside main population centres. It shows, too, comparative levels of popularity for different art forms and events. Such data could feed into future planning, though the assumption might not be simply to even out the availability of provision – there might be specific historical or geographical reasons for a particular high or low occurrence of participation. Having said that, however, just as *Window Sills* and the workshops at St Adrià de Besòs fuse qualitative and quantitative methods - we would say inevitably in the realities of the practices concerned – so the more orthodox evaluation of Visions of Utopia includes qualitative material alongside statistics. Indeed, it is the extracts from user responses which illuminate this report. In the particular case of the project with the Probation Service, in which, for obvious reasons, participants remain anonymous in the evaluation report delivered to Helix Arts, their voices nonetheless articulate the worth of the project in a way numbers cannot. And here, too, is unpredictability. The hope is that young offenders will gain in self worth and thereby be less likely to re-offend. But only after several years and tracking of all participants – a fraught exercise – could data be produced. It is also difficult to quantify the cost savings involved in as yet uncommitted crimes not being committed. This is unlikely to stop funding bodies using such arguments to government. The point though, we maintain, is ethical: that people who have special needs or are in marginal or disadvantaged circumstances deserve, as human subjects, humane treatment. The arts probably contribute to this but the evidence remains largely anecdotal.

An equally open-ended question is whether external evaluators can produce knowledge of a project's reception which is of a greater value or use than that provided from its own initiators. An argument would, of course, be that outsiders with suitable professional experience see a project's impact more objectively than those who have a vested interest in its being seen as a success. Both *Window Sills* and *Visions of Utopia* employed external consultants. *Platform* too, have (beyond the scope of the project described above) recently undertaken a lengthy period of self-analysis facilitated by a consultant, and informed by the consultant's independent investigation of Platform's perception by those who have contact with it. Consultants are numerous today, but to employ them is a significant additional cost to a project. Is it worth it?

Our impression from all the cases is that working with (rather than being distantly observed by) external consultants does have advantages. But they may not be the obvious ones. Our position is speculative but we advance it: the anecdotal material included in the report on *Visions of Utopia* might as easily and we feel accurately have been produced by staff at Helix Arts. Particularly, long-serving staff tend to have reasonably objective views of their own activities, and discuss projects among themselves accordingly, because they realise that inaccurate or wishful views are unhelpful. Merely knowing what took place, then, is not the point. It is more that working with an external investigator leads those who do so to focus on what they are doing in a different and probably more articulated way. This is what might be the main value, apart from producing the reports funding bodies may require or trust. A second advantage is in gaining assistance in collating and interpreting the findings of an evaluation. In the case of *Window Sills*, a researcher within the project carried out most of the evaluation, but the findings were clarified through selective engagement with an external consultant. For the project in Santt Adrià de Besòs a similar function may have been carried out by the city authorities with whom the University's researchers have regular contact and (now) increasing collaboration.

The comparison of the four cases raises a sub-issue here: the extent to which projects are seen as art or social process; and how far either can or cannot be evaluated objectively. In the case of *Killing Us Softly*, the aim of feedback is for the lead artist (Dan Gretton) to refine his performance and the way he orders his (increasingly vast body of) material. It is useful for him to know, colloquially, what works and what does not; but also what questions and associations participants produce themselves during, or – perhaps especially – in reflection after an event. But this is quite close to the idea of a practitioner who develops a practice through critical reflection: a standard art school model and in its way reliant on the autonomy claimed for modern art. The art produced in *Window Sills*, whatever its community focus, is also art in the conventional sense of work made by (if with others) professional artists trained in art schools. The artists in the calendar project in *Visions of Utopia* were young offenders, a few of whom may go to art school. But they are non-professionals and the project's key concern is with social conditions and human dynamics. Similarly, the workshops in Sant Adrià de Besòs were facilitated by professionals and academics but to a significant extent 'owned' by dwellers. It may be that different means of evaluation are required. If so, to evaluate a social process is likely to be outside the skill base of an arts consultant, more the domain of political scientists, sociologists or ethnographers.

This leads neatly into discussion of anecdotal and statistical knowledge. At the most obvious level, knowing that 3,000 people attended a concert does not say anything about what they experienced or why they went. It says that an event was successful, perhaps, in an auditable way but it does not say if anyone experienced a shift of consciousness (or wanted to). We suggest that anecdotal information, despite its tendency to exaggeration and mythicisation, particular as time lapses, is vital. It is the stories people tell of something that constitute its reality as a factor in wider social development. Experience is private but its expression is public. If art can contribute to social change, it is probably through its ability to nudge in new directions the ways in which people think about their lives, themselves and the world in which they live with others. This can only be accessed through anecdotal information, through extended conversations and the like.

Anecdotal information is, in any case, widely used in the social sciences and radical planning. The radical planner hangs out with the mobilised community group to gain insight into their needs and aspirations which can be communicated within the planning process. The urban ethnographer — and much ethnography is carried out in the researcher's own country, not now in exotic places — hangs out with selected members of a social group, gaining their confidence before learning very much about their values and ways of organising their spaces and routines. If the social sciences have tested methodologies for dealing with such material, which figures frequently in doctoral theses alongside more conventional kinds of data, then arts evaluation should have no problem in approaching it. No problem, that is, except that arts evaluators are not usually educated as social scientists. There seems a strong case, then, for a more multi-disciplinary approach to evaluation in the arts in non-institutional settings.

Is it, then, useful to measure reception? Firstly, without the demands of some kind of evaluative process, the pressures of survival in a small arts organisation, or for individual artists, might well dictate that in-depth reflection does not take place. The short-termism of most arts funding bodies tends to make artists peripatetic and to chase future budgets rather than think back on past projects. There is also some pressure to be confident and appear outwardly a success, which may inhibit genuine criticism. Platform is highly unusual in the amount of time and resource it devotes to documentation and feedback and has a policy of setting its own agenda rather than following those of arts funders. *Visions of Utopia* had the benefit of being organised by an agency with long-term roots in the region and well-established links to public-sector agencies and authorities. *Window Sills* and the work in Sant Adrià de Besòs had the advantage of being housed by university departments, which also provide some respite from day-to-day searches for cash (though not entirely in today's increasingly market-led provision of higher education). Secondly, it is necessary for public money to be accounted for. However rudimentary are the means to do so, projects paid by the public purse should be open to independent evaluation. This is less to ensure the money is properly spent – there are very few instances of corruption – as to feed lessons into future funding strategies and wider cultural policies. The status of an external evaluation, as for *Visions of Utopia*, may be higher in this respect than one carried out internally. At the same time, the questions asked by artists - the actors in the situation – and institutions – parts of the structure – will differ.

It is difficult to sum up from four different projects managed in different ways and with different aims. The long-term impact of each is hard to estimate – and the quality of experience of an individual may outweigh the quantity of participation. But that qualitative experience is private, may or may not be communicated to a researcher. It may take either a short or a long time to become evident even for the participant – sometimes it is when several events coincide in memory that an insight occurs. Ultimately, all four projects are about people gaining realisation of their human potential – in that way utopian, in a society which has many well-tested mechanisms to stop such realisation. This is nebulous and not measurable as such. But what can be ascertained, in a mix of formal and informal approaches, is whether a specific project delivered something meaningful enough to engage, in fact to create, a public for it. This is not measured by numbers because publics can consist of a few individuals with some common cause; but it can be identified through straightforward means of interview, focus group and conversation. And it can be more fully articulated when an external evaluator is involved or when collaboration takes place with other agencies.

Finally, then, an old saying is that all research leads to identification of new needs for research. In this case, we draw attention to:
- the need to use a more multi-disciplinary approach to evaluation, which not only suits the means of investigation to the subject under investigation but also draws on relevant experience in non-art disciplines;
- the need to look again at the relation between arts policy, funding strategies and modes of evaluation so that these are not contradictory or fanciful;
- the need to support arts organisations and universities in collaborating with each other both in delivering projects and in evaluating them.

Bibliography

Adams, D. and Goldbard, A. (2001) *Creative Community:The Art of Cultural Development*. New York: Rockfeller Foundation.

Bennett, S. and Butler, J. (2000) *Locality, Regeneration and Divers[c]ities*. Bristol: Intellect

Durland S, (1998) The Citizen Artist, Gardiner, New York: Critical Press

Farley, R and Casman, S. (1999) *Visions of Utopia*. Evaluation report. Newcastle: University of Northumbria.

Farley, R. (1999) *Futurelives Indifferentspaces*. Evaluation report. Newcastle: University of Northumbria.

Kelly, A. and Kelly, M. (2000) *Impact and Values – Assessing the Arts and Creative Industries in the South West*. Bristol: Bristol Cultural Development Partnership.

Landry, C. (2000) *The Creative City*. London: Lifescan.

Matarasso, F. (1997) *Use or Ornament? The Social Impact of Participation in the Arts*. Stroud: Comedia

Mosely, P. (1998) *Evaluation: A guide devised to support the arts Council of England's Artists in Sites for Learning scheme*. Arts Council England.

Rorty, R. (1989) *Contingency, Irony and Solidarity*. Cambridge: Cambridge University Press.

Selwood, S. (1995) *The Benefits of Public Art*. London: Policy Studies Institute.

Shaw, P. (1999) *Policy Action Team 10 Research Report: Arts and Neighbourhood Renewal*. Department for Culture, Media and Sport.

Social Exclusion Unit (1998) Bringing Britain Back Together: A National Strategy for Neighbourhood Renewal, London: Stationary Office.

Williams, J. (2001)*Window Sills, an Independent Evaluation*. Centre for Creative Communities: unpublished.

Woolf, F. (1999) *Partnerships for Learning: a guide to evaluating arts education partnerships*. London: Arts Council England.

Notes

1   The City Port Territory group changed its name to Environmental Intervention: Art, City & Sustainability when the group led by Dr. Enric Pol joined the project. Later on this group became the promoter of the Polis Research Centre at the University of Barcelona (1999).

2   See CER POLIS Environmental Intervention : Art, City & Sustainability website www.ub.es/escult/1.htm

3   Unattributed quotes and views on this project are from a conversation with Esther Salamon, 25 – 26 November 1999, and subsequent telephone contact.

Tim Hall and Chereen Smith

Public Art in the City: Meanings, Values, Attitudes and Roles

Introduction

Some writers have argued that since the 1980s the cities of Europe, the USA and beyond have witnessed a 'renaissance' of public art (Moody, 1990: 2), characterised by a rise in public and private sector commissions, an expansion of arts policy and administrative structures and an increasing integration of artists into the urban design process. Much of this has been fuelled by the international growth of 'percent for arts' policies amongst local authorities. Public art has now become closely associated with the regeneration of cities, the aesthetic enhancement of urban environments and promoting tangible improvements to people's lives. Public art, then, is becoming an increasingly ubiquitous and prominent feature of urban landscapes and is said to be fulfilling a number of roles in the economic, social and cultural regeneration of these places.

This has not gone unnoticed by writers, critics and researchers. However, despite growing bodies of critical writing, there remain a number of significant gaps and omissions. Most seriously, no one has made a sustained attempt to discover if the responses of urban residents to public art and the values they attach to it correspond with the widely advocated roles for public art in the city. Evidence collected to date, therefore, is insufficient to demonstrate the full range of the impacts of public art, their limitations or to properly inform policy and strategy.

This chapter aims to broadly outline the context within which a new research project on public art has been commissioned to make a substantive attempt to examine public art through its audiences, and provides an overview of the proposed methodological approaches. This research project is concerned with uncovering the meanings and responses of urban residents to public art and will establish more precisely therefore, the actual impacts of public art and its spaces in their everyday lives and discover the extent to which these correspond with the widely advocated roles for public art.

The Claims of Public Art

Public art has long been advocated on the basis that it can improve the quality of people's lives. In the context of urban regeneration, a number of specific claims have been made about it. Through a review based largely on published accounts of public projects, Hall and Robertson (2001) identified six such claims upon which it is argued that public art can:

- promote a sense of community and an awareness of local cultural identity
- promote the development of social networks and tackle social exclusion
- promote senses of place and the connections between communities and places

- develop and promote civic identity
- have an educative function
- act as a provocation for social change

In addition we can recognise three intermediate outcomes through which, it is argued, these impacts are achieved. It has been claimed that public art:
- aesthetically enhances environments
- acts as a medium for the communication of symbolic meanings
- acts as a vehicle for participatory and co-operative activity

It has long been argued that the aesthetic improvements associated with public art projects have a number of social impacts, for example, promoting senses of community amongst residents of disadvantaged neighbourhoods. Advocates argue that public art can improve the spaces of public culture and social interaction, increase senses of security and reduce fear of public space. Thus, it is often claimed that public art can 'humanise' prosaic urban forms (Duffin, 1993; Dunlop, 1995).

The symbolic meanings of public art are said to affect a number of impacts. Most obviously they can refer to spatial, cultural and social identities. The iconographies of public art works might explore notions of identity or the histories of neighbourhoods, towns and cities. Some have argued that such iconographies can be active in the formation of social identities. In addition it has been argued that the themes and contents of arts projects 'give affirmation to diverse cultures and traditions' (Blaney, 1989: 83). Further, projects might draw attention to issues of local concern within marginalized communities and communicate them externally. Thus Blaney concludes, 'art can be a stimulus for alienated people and can serve as the first step in the ladder towards their full participation in society' (1989: 83).

Participation in public art projects has been said to produce a wide range of direct and indirect benefits (Matarasso, 1997), as outlined previously, for example, contributing to the development of social networks and reducing social exclusion.

Investigating Public Art's Audiences

Public art has become an increasingly debated subject across a range of disciplines. Much critical literature on public art has emanated from cultural studies and cultural geography and has reflected the approaches dominant in these disciplines. These include a concern for the politics of representation and interpretative approaches that attempt to 'read', 'unpack' or 'deconstruct' the meanings of cultural texts (see for example, Hall, 1997a; 1997b; Miles, 1997; 1998). Whist these approaches offer 'sophisticated methods of saying a great deal about art they are able to say very little about the public', missing the crucial and complex audience dimension (Hall and Robinson, 2001:19).

'Investigations of audiences are very well developed in disciplines such as cultural and media studies, however a concern with audiences is less well developed in urban geography. Studies of architecture, urban landscapes and spaces have focused far more on the production and text than they have on audience'. Investigations of audiences of visual texts raise questions about studies that focus on other sites of meaning by recognising that there is no necessary correspondence between the intended meanings of the author(s) or producer(s) of text and those constructed by audiences.

Emergent debates within urban studies and cultural geography have, however, increasingly begun to emphasise the importance of the consumption or construction of meanings of landscape by urban publics, calling for research to move away from an overriding concern with representation and interpretation and an associated focus on the sites of production and text (see for example Thrift 2000, Mitchell, 1995). Whilst there is evidence that geographers are beginning to take on board calls to include audiences in their research (see for example Lees, 2001; Burgess et. al, 1988) there has, to date, been little attempt to investigate the audiences of public art or the significance of public art to the everyday lives of urban publics. The wealth of sophisticated theoretical writing about the production of public art and the symbolic meanings of public artworks stands in stark contrast to the dearth of writing about its audiences. Neither the intentions of the producers of public art, nor its iconographies necessarily correspond to the meanings derived from the incorporation of public art and its spaces into the everyday lives of urban residents. One simple, yet important, question emerges from this. To what extent do the sophisticated readings of public art offered by various cultural theorists correspond to those meanings constructed by its audiences?

The difficulty in answering this question adequately suggests limitations in previous writing on public art and untapped avenues of investigation. In addition this raises questions for arts advocates, developers and artists. Again, put simply, we know little about the extent to which the bases upon which public art is advocated and developed correspond to the experiences of public art and the attitudes towards it held by urban residents. Intriguingly, other chapters in this collection offer many glimpses.

Some research efforts have been made recently to capture the responses of audiences of public art (programmes) adopting a variety of techniques, including, an action research project undertaken by a co-operative enquiry group with art professionals, commissioned by the Arts Council England that sought to 'initiate a critical engagement, through practice, concerning the workings of public art' (Arts Council England, 2003); an artist-led 'soft' research project, which encouraged Milton Keynes residents to 'look anew at the artwork in their city', commissioned by Artpoint (2003); and a research project, conducted by a commercial research group, that initiated one-off focus group interviews with residents to 'find out what the public needs in order to appreciate, find and make use of public art in Westminster' (Westcombe Business Research Ltd. 1998). The earlier work of Sara Selwood (1995) also incorporated some element of attitudes of different publics in her multi-dimensional evaluation of the claims of public art. However this did not extend much beyond the use of structured surveys and the analysis of press discourse.

Whilst the undertakings of these and similar research projects go some way to redressing the bias in much critical literature, this is still in its infancy. Research to date has largely been commissioned to address internal inquiries or aimed to encourage those involved in public art, social art practice and audience research to reflect on the many assumptions of their professions. There is as yet little by way of developed procedures or critical theoretical frameworks within this public art research that adequately addresses the omission of voices into research and salient debates.

The failure of critical writing of public art to examine seriously its audiences, their experiences and the meanings they construct has therefore prompted the commissioning of a new research project on public art to examine the social and cultural geographies of public art from the perspective of its audiences.

The Research

The methodological approach proposed for this piece of empirical, qualitative research displays a sensitivity to the language, beliefs, attitudes, values and behaviours of urban residents. This will be addressed through three research questions:
- What roles does public art play in the everyday lives of urban residents?
- What values do urban residents attach to public art?
- In what ways, and to what extent, do these behaviours, beliefs, attitudes and values vary socially?

The research will examine the attitudes of residents of one city, Birmingham, to public art in their city. Birmingham has a tradition of civic statuary dating back to the Victorian era. It developed a number of high profile programmes of public art in the 1980s and 1990s in association with the extensive regeneration of the city's central areas (Hall, 1997). The city has a number of other public art projects, in a variety of contrasting neighbourhoods throughout the city (Noszlopy, 1998). The decision to use Birmingham in this research was based on the variety of public art within the city and the centrality of public art projects to recent projects of urban regeneration, and on the other hand, to build upon the wide variety of research that has already been undertaken on the regeneration of the centre of Birmingham and the position that public art has assumed within this (Hall, 1994; 1995; 1997; Sargent, 1996).

With the intention to uncover the readings of public art and its landscapes and spaces by the individuals and groups who encounter them, the first research stage involves a series of focus group interviews with residents of Birmingham, during which their perception, experiences and attitudes to public art in their city will be examined. Focus groups are an appropriate method because they offer a setting within which people can talk freely about individual and shared experiences and develop a group dynamic that reveals both manifest and latent meanings (Burgess et. al, 1988: 458). Through carefully planned discussions, focus groups aim to 'expose differences, contradictions and, in short, the complexity of unique experiences' (Bennett, 2002:151).

Five groups in total will be constituted from contrasting neighbourhoods, demonstrating differing socio-economic characteristics, ethnic mix and housing type, with each group meeting on three occasions. Each set of group interviews will be based around an interview schedule, spread across the three meetings. This will aim to provide *'sufficient structure to ensure that the group continues to address the research topic while not inhibiting the natural flow of group interaction'* (Bloor et. al, 2001:43). A small number of broadly focused, open-ended questions are designed to invite participants to 'explore the topic in a way that generates new insights' (Morgan, 1998:45).

Between the first and second focus group meetings the participants will each be given a disposable camera and asked to produce a series of photographs that reflect their views and attitudes about public art. They will be invited to use these photographs to produce a collage at a subsequent meeting. Self-directed photography and collage production will both act as prompts to discussion and as cultural texts in themselves that can be interrogated to reveal attitudes towards public art. Self-directed photography has a long tradition within social research and has been used in studies of people's attitudes to the urban environment (Aitken and Wingate, 1993). However, its potential has not been fully realised and it has never been used to explore attitudes towards public art. The project will demonstrate that lay visual knowledges can act as important sources in studies of the urban landscape. Photography acts as a discourse between producer, subject and viewer. Rather than representing a mimetic reflection of reality, it represents an actively constructed cultural text that can be deconstructed both through discussion with producer and viewer and through semiotic analysis.

Each group interview will be tape recorded with the permission of the participants, and once transcribed, the group discussions will be interpreted and cross-referenced. Tape recording is the most appropriate method, as the primary source of recording at least, as it captures the 'subtlety of language and nuances of meaning that would otherwise have been lost in a crude summary of the events' and allows for a 'much finer textual analysis' (Burgess et. al, 1988a:320). More importantly, a verbatim record of each group enables critical evaluation of the researchers own performances in the production of the data, the influences of which, it is argued, too often remain hidden within research (Burgess et. al, 1988a:320).

The analysis will focus on the exploration of themes held by individuals and groups of participants. This will be followed by the production of reports summarising the main findings of the group interviews.

Summary

Whist the subject of public art has become an increasingly debated subject across a wide range of disciplines, it has tended to reflect approaches that are concerned overwhelmingly on the production of public art and on the symbolic meanings of public artworks. However, concerned with uncovering the meanings and responses of urban residents to public art, this new research project will establish more precisely the actual impacts of public art and its spaces in their everyday lives and discover the extent to which these correspond with the widely advocated roles for public art. This research will therefore not only contribute to emergent debates within urban studies and cultural geography but additionally stands to advance our understanding of public art, breaking new ground in the study of public art and intended to make major contributions to debates around the study of public art.

Bibliography

Aitken, S. C. and Wingate, J. (1993) A preliminary study of the self-directed photography of middle-class, homeless, and mobility-impaired children, *The Professional Geographer*, 45(1), 65-72.

Artpoint (2002) Personal Views: Responding to and Researching Public Art in Milton Keynes, www.publicartonline.org.uk/news/research/personal_views_mk.html accessed 11/11/03

Arts Council England (2003) West Midlands Launches Audentis — a new website investigating public art, www.artscouncilenglad.org.uk 12/06/2003 accessed 11/10/03

Bennett, K. (2002) Interviews and Focus Groups, in Shurmer-Smith, P. (ed.)(2002) *Doing Cultural Geography*. London SAGE Publications. London.

Blaney, J. (1989) The arts and the development of community in suburbia in British and American Arts Association (eds.) *Arts and the Changing City: An Agenda for Urban Regeneration*. London: British and American Arts Association.

Bloor, M., Frankland, J., Thomas, M., Robson, K. (2001) *Focus Groups in Social Research; Introducing Qualitative Methods*. London: SAGE Publications, London.

Burgess, J., Limb, M. and Harrison, C. M (1988) People, Parks and the Urban Green: A Study of Popular Meanings and Values for Open Spaces in the City. *Urban Studies*, vol. 25, pp. 455–473.

Burgess, J., Limb, M, and Harrison, C. M (1988a) Exploring environmental values through the medium of small groups: 1. Theory and practice, *Environment and Planning A*, vol. 20, pp. 209–326.

Duffin, D. (1993) A Model City. *Artists Newsletter*, March, pp. 16–19.

Dunlop J. (1995) Beyond Decoration *Artists Newsletter*, June 26–29.

Hall, T. (1995) Public art, urban image. *Town and Country Planner* 64, 4, pp. 122–123.

Hall, T. (1997a) Images of industry in the post-industrial city: Raymond Mason and Birmingham, *Ecumene* 4 1, pp. 46–68.

Hall, T. (1997b) (Re)placing the city: Cultural relocation and the city as centre in Westwood, S. and Williams, J. (eds.) *Imagining Cities: Scripts, Signs, and Memories*. London: Routledge, pp. 202–218.

Hall, T. and Robinson (2001) Public art and urban regeneration: Advocacy, claims and critical debates *Landscape Research* 26 1, pp. 5–26.

Hall, T. (2003) Art and Urban Change: Public Art in Urban Regeneration in Blunt, A. Gruffud, P. May, J. Ogborn, M. and Pinder, D. (eds.) *Cultural Geography in Practice*. London: Arnold.

Lees, L. (2001) Towards a critical geography of architecture: The case of an ersatz colosseum, *Ecumene* 8, 1, pp. 51–86.

Matarasso, F. (1997) Use or Ornament? The Social Impact of Participation in the Arts Comedia. Stroud.

Miles, M. (1997) *Art, Space and the City* London: Routledge.

Miles, M. (1998) A game of appearance: public art in urban development, complicity or sustainability? In Hall, T. and Hubbard, P. (eds.) *The Entrepreneurial City: Geographies of Politics, Regime and Representation*. Chichester: John Wiley, pp. 203–224.

Mitchell, R.(1995) 'There's no such thing as culture'. *Transactions of the Institute of British Geographers* 20, pp. 102–116.

Moody, E. (1990) Introduction in Public Art Forum Public Art Report Public Art forum, London eds. pp. 2–3.

Morgan, D. L.(1998) *Planning Focus Groups*, London: SAGE Publications.

Nozlopsy, G. and Beach, J. (1998) Public Sculpture of Birmingham. University of Liverpool Press: Liverpool.

Sargent, A. (1996) More than just the sum of its parts: Cultural policy and planning in Birmingham, *Cultural Policy* 2, 2, pp. 303–325

Selwood, S. (1992) Art in Public, in Jones, S.(ed.) (1992) Art in Public: What, Why and How. Sunderland: AN Publications.

Thrift, N. (2000) Non-representational theory in Johnstone, R. Gregory, D. Pratt, G. and Watts, M. (eds.) *The Dictionary of Human Geography*, 4th ed. Oxford: Blackwell, pp. 556.

Westcombe Business Research Limited. (1998) *Promoting Public Art Project: Qualitative Research Project*. Westcombe Business Research Limited.